ISSUE 7, OCTOBER 2019

AUSTRALIAN FOREIGN AFFAIRS

Contributors   2

Editor's Note   3

Allan Gyngell
History Hasn't Ended   5

Margaret Simons
High Price   28

Richard McGregor
Trade Deficits   54

David Uren
Hostile Takeover   75

Special Report
Ben Bohane on Bougainville's Quest for Independence   99

The Fix
Melissa Conley Tyler on How to Rebuild Australia's Diplomatic Capacity   109

Reviews
David Kilcullen *How to Defend Australia* by Hugh White   117
Astrid Edwards *The Uninhabitable Earth* by David Wallace-Wells   123
David Fettling *Race, Islam and Power* by Andreas Harsono   127
Greg Earl *Peak Japan* by Brad Glosserman   132

Correspondence
"In Denial": Jonathan Pryke, Wesley Morgan; response by Hugh White   136
"Cross Purposes": Sandra Tarte, Paul Ronalds, Carlisle Richardson; response by Jenny Hayward-Jones   145

The Back Page by Richard Cooke   160

Contributors

Ben Bohane is a Vanuatu-based photojournalist, producer and policy analyst.

Melissa Conley Tyler is director of diplomacy at Asialink at the University of Melbourne.

Greg Earl was *The Australian Financial Review*'s Japan correspondent and a board member of the Australia–Japan Foundation.

Astrid Edwards hosts *The Garret* podcast and teaches at RMIT University.

David Fettling is a journalist focusing on South-East Asia and an AFA Next Voices winner.

Allan Gyngell is national president of the Australian Institute of International Affairs and an honorary professor at the Australian National University.

David Kilcullen is professor of international and political studies at the University of New South Wales and a contributing editor at *The Australian*.

Richard McGregor is a senior fellow for East Asia at the Lowy Institute.

Margaret Simons is a board member of the Public Interest Journalism Initiative and an associate professor at Monash University.

David Uren was economics editor of *The Australian* and is the author of *Takeover* and *The Kingdom and the Quarry*.

Australian Foreign Affairs is published three times a year by Schwartz Books Pty Ltd. Publisher: Morry Schwartz. ISBN 978-1-76064-1665 ISSN 2208-5912 ALL RIGHTS RESERVED. No part of this publication may be reproduced, stored in a retrieval system, or transmitted in any form by any means, electronic, mechanical, photocopying, recording or otherwise, without the prior consent of the publishers. Essays, reviews and correspondence © retained by the authors. Subscriptions – 1 year print & digital auto-renew (3 issues): $49.99 within Australia incl. GST. 1 year print and digital subscription (3 issues): $59.99 within Australia incl. GST. 2 year print & digital (6 issues): $114.99 within Australia incl. GST. 1 year digital only auto-renew: $29.99. Payment may be made by MasterCard, Visa or Amex, or by cheque made out to Schwartz Books Pty Ltd. Payment includes postage and handling. To subscribe, fill out the form inside this issue, subscribe online at www.australianforeignaffairs.com, email subscribe@australianforeignaffairs.com or phone 1800 077 514 / 61 3 9486 0288. Correspondence should be addressed to: The Editor, Australian Foreign Affairs, Level 1, 221 Drummond Street, Carlton VIC 3053 Australia Phone: 61 3 9486 0288 / Fax: 61 3 9486 0244 Email: enquiries@australianforeignaffairs.com Editor: Jonathan Pearlman. Associate Editor: Chris Feik. Consulting Editor: Allan Gyngell. Deputy Editor: Julia Carlomagno. *AFA Weekly* Editor: Dion Kagan. Editorial Intern: Lachlan McIntosh. Management: Elisabeth Young. Marketing: Georgia Mill and Iryna Byelyayeva. Publicity: Anna Lensky. Design: Peter Long. Production Coordination: Marilyn de Castro. Typesetting: Akiko Chan. Cover photograph of containers by narvikk/Getty Images. Printed in Australia by McPherson's Printing Group.

Editor's Note

CHINA DEPENDENCE

On 6 May 2008 Australia declared that China was now its largest trading partner. This development had actually occurred in 2007, but it was only announced by trade minister Simon Crean once annual figures had been released. Still, Crean was reserved: "Japan will continue to be Australia's largest export destination for the foreseeable future."

A year later, China overtook Japan as Australia's largest export market. China now accounts for 40 per cent of Australian exports – more than the combined total of the next three countries: Japan, the United States and South Korea. No other developed country is as reliant on trade with China – especially not the United States, which has less to lose from a Chinese downturn. This puts Australia in an unusual position. Countries that have been central to Australia's economy, such as Britain, the United States and Japan, all share similar geopolitical outlooks. China views Asia's power balance differently, and is increasingly capable of reshaping it.

For Australia, this is causing deep anxieties. The worry is that political or diplomatic disagreements with China will prompt it to suddenly disrupt the flow of iron ore, or coal, or students, or tourists. Or that it will misuse its growing presence and assets in Australia. Security and economics are tugging Canberra in different directions, as are its values and its interests.

The first challenge is to understand how China operates, and whether Australia is at risk. In the past two years, relations with Beijing have arguably been worse than at any time since the Tiananmen Square massacre in 1989. The two countries have disagreed over Australia's foreign interference laws, the pro-democracy protests in Hong Kong, the mass detention of Uyghur Muslims and China's arrests of Chinese-Australians. Yet trade has soared. China also has its dependencies, and would suffer if, say, it lost its most reliable iron ore supplier. But China's willingness to use its trade clout could change, particularly if ties with Australia deteriorate due to its US partnership.

The second challenge is to adapt to this new predicament. Politicians need to consider how to sensibly handle their differences with Beijing. Businesses need to look at whether investment from China poses security risks, and universities at how their student influx affects their financial risk and the campus experience.

The best hope for the nation's stability is that China remains our top trading partner. Australia should do all it can to ensure the mutual benefits from the relationship continue, that the costs and risks are contained, and that any future fallout has been anticipated.

Jonathan Pearlman

HISTORY HASN'T ENDED

How to handle China

Allan Gyngell

In April, Kiron Skinner, until recently head of policy planning in the US State Department and a successor to the legendary George F. Kennan, architect of America's Cold War strategy of containment, described US relations with China as "a fight with a really different civilisation" and the "first time we will have a great power competitor that is not Caucasian".

Her critics, understandably, piled on. Had she forgotten whose aircraft attacked Pearl Harbor? What did race have to do with great power competition? Didn't the Marxism–Leninism of the Chinese Communist Party (CCP) emerge from Western roots?

But Skinner's comments were a revealing acknowledgement by a senior US policymaker of how China's distinctiveness is shaping Western responses to its rise. America has never faced a peer competitor such as this.

In Australia, fears of Asian difference shaped strategic and social policy for much of the twentieth century. The White Australia policy was one of its dismal manifestations. And it was indeed a threat from Asia in 1942 that provided the biggest challenge of the nation's history. My professional life began in a world in which anxiety about Chinese communist expansionism dominated foreign policy discussions and Australian diplomats in Asia could not speak to their Mao-suited Chinese counterparts, whose government we did not recognise until 1972.

But for forty years now, since Deng Xiaoping began China's economic reforms and advised his country to "hide its capability and bide its time", Australia has sailed through magic decades in which, as our leaders regularly intoned, we did not have to choose between our prosperity and our security. John Howard could welcome the US and Chinese presidents to address the Australian parliament on successive days in 2003.

Those days have gone. And for Australia, the sense of strangeness is growing.

We have never had to manage a relationship as important as the one we have with China, with a country so different in its language, culture, history and values. Nor one with an Asian state so confident, and possessing so many dimensions of power. Japan may have been the world's second-largest economy, but in strategic terms it was a client of the United States.

Even at its current slower pace, China's GDP is growing each year by roughly the equivalent of the entire Australian economy.

Our government's own projections see it surpassing the United States in total economic size (though not per capita income or comprehensive power) by the end of the next decade.

Under Xi Jinping's leadership, China has become less open and more tightly controlled. Aided by new technologies such as artificial intelligence, the party-state has tightened social control throughout the country, especially over groups such as the Muslim Uyghur minority, which it deems a threat. China's foreign policy has become more assertive, displaying ambitions that challenge the established regional order. Its military forces have been reorganised and reformed. Defence spending rose by more than 80 per cent between 2009 and 2018.

Can the ambitions of a growing China be reconciled with Australia's national interests and values?

Australia's relationship with China has domestic as well as international dimensions. It affects our budget sustainability, foreign investment, the viability of our universities and social cohesion. More than 1.2 million Australians claim Chinese ancestry, and we have seen growing evidence of People's Republic of China (PRC) efforts to influence Australian institutions and policy debates. Canberra has become a more anxious town. Anyone who knows the place understands how quickly a sensible centrist consensus forms among the public servants, policy advisers, academics and think-tankers who make up the country's foreign policy establishment. That consensus can be wrong (see weapons of mass destruction in Iraq) but it has underpinned a system in which the serious fights were over bureaucratic resources rather than the policies to deal with the world.

China is testing the consensus. The debate is getting sharper. Commentators and analysts from the think tanks and universities are marshalling themselves into hostile camps. Those arguing for engagement with China risk being dismissed as agents of influence or naive tools of Beijing. On the other side, suspicions of security agency conspiracies run deep, reinforced by a pattern of leaks to journalists. The business community mostly wants clarity in a situation that can't deliver it.

The challenge we face with China isn't having to choose between our economy and our security. It's more difficult than that. We have to find a path that enables us to protect and manage both. At the same time, the decisions are coming faster – whether to approve particular investment proposals; how to respond to the Belt and Road Initiative; what to do about challenges to maritime law in the South China Sea; how to react to demonstrations in Hong Kong.

At the core of these choices lies one basic question: can the ambitions of a growing China be reconciled with Australia's national interests and values? To answer that, we need to be as clear as we can about what China wants, and about how we define our interests and values.

The Chinese dream

What *does* China want? The "Chinese dream", Xi told the nineteenth Communist Party Congress, is one of national rejuvenation in an era "that sees China move close to the centre stage and making great contributions to mankind". China's goal is to become a state "with substantial global influence".

Xi and his colleagues emphasise the CCP's indispensability in achieving that dream, but the broad objective – a China moving beyond the humiliations of the nineteenth and twentieth centuries to a place of influence commensurate with its history and culture – is one that a large majority of Chinese citizens share.

Like all large powers – like all countries – China wants to shape a world more conducive to its interests, one in which it can attain its objectives at a minimum cost. Beijing's frustrations with the constraints of some dimensions of the global order have become clear. With initiatives such as the Asian Infrastructure Investment Bank (AIIB), it is building institutions that suit its interests and priorities. Ignoring international tribunal rulings, it has reinforced its control over disputed territories in the South China Sea and, contrary to Xi's promises, militarised islands it occupies there, as part of a broader effort to counter US military dominance in East Asia. Through the Belt and Road Initiative, it is using its economic strength to deepen its influence over its neighbours and trade partners and to mould new standards and norms.

It is stepping into areas Australia regards as within its own sphere of influence. "We are committed by inexorable circumstances to the doctrine 'Hands off the Pacific'," declared the Australian prime minister – not Scott Morrison, but Billy Hughes, in 1919. Hughes had Japan rather than China in mind, but the idea that outside intrusions into the South West Pacific represent a strategic threat has deep roots in our thinking about the world.

It is not surprising that China has shrugged off Deng Xiaoping's "hide and bide" advice. That was a useful policy for a weak state, but it's hardly a plausible approach for the world's second-largest economy.

Yet the pace of change in China can sometimes distort our perception of its scale. Claims like those in the 2018 US National Defense Strategy – the Pentagon's first such blueprint since 2008 – that Beijing is seeking "Indo-Pacific regional hegemony in the near term and displacement of the United States to achieve global pre-eminence in the future" are overblown.

Discounting official Chinese pronouncements about the modesty of its national aims, and even accepting that world domination may be the secret desire of some People's Liberation Army generals and nationalist think-tankers, "near-term regional hegemony" in the Indo-Pacific (presumably meaning the swathe of the world covered by the US Indo-Pacific Command) is an implausible ambition for the Beijing government. America's US$733 billion defence budget is still greater than those of the next eight countries in the world combined.

China faces significant challenges. These include an ageing population, problems of labour productivity, growing local government debt, environmental degradation and water shortages. Tens of millions of Chinese still live in poverty. To sustain its legitimacy in the face of these challenges, the CCP leadership is still more likely to see its interests served by a stable geopolitical and economic environment than by risky confrontation.

There is no blueprint for China's future. The ambitions of its government will be formed over time by the strength of its economy, the foresight and resolution of its leaders, the skill of its diplomacy and the responses of other states. Of those, none matters more than the United States.

The US pivot from China

America's complementarity with China may have ended, but Australia's has not

Australia's growing uncertainty about the future of its relationship with China is not only due to China's changing behaviour. It stems as much from the United States' speedy and bipartisan decision to reframe its relationship with Beijing.

The historic meeting between Richard Nixon and Mao Zedong in 1972 took place at a time when CCP rule was bloodier and more repressive than anything we see now. But notwithstanding their different systems, Washington's geopolitical interests aligned with Beijing's against the Soviet Union.

Later, after China's reforms began, the two countries discovered complementary economic interests. China provided cheap production facilities and new markets for US companies, dramatically lowering the cost of consumer goods in America. In return, it had access to the investment flows and markets of the world's richest economy.

But by the end of the first decade of this century, that had changed. China continued to grow, and its actions, including cyber-theft and the hoovering up of intellectual property, harmed American interests and frustrated its business community. It became clear that China was no longer prepared to accept a role as a simple stakeholder in a system designed by Washington. Beijing began to challenge America's leadership in East Asia and the world, and its primacy in areas of advanced technology that underpinned its strategic dominance.

In response, the United States put behind it the messiness of the War on Terror and the failure of its Middle East interventions and embraced, with some sense of national relief, a return to the arena of great power competition. In the words of the journalist Martin Wolf, "across-the-board rivalry with China is becoming an organising principle of US economic, financial and security policies".

American concern about China predates the Trump administration. It was President Obama who initiated the Asian "pivot", including the rotation of US marines through Darwin, and promoted the Trans-Pacific Partnership trade agreement. No Democrat presidential candidate in 2020 will want to risk being soft on China.

Perhaps the two countries will move towards a Cold War–like confrontation, competing globally across all the dimensions of power, with an ever-present risk of military conflict. Or we might see a mutually agreed separation, wary but not always antagonistic, involving a managed decoupling of the two economies and a return to national technological walled gardens. Or maybe the PRC will come to understand that China can prosper best if it accommodates the security and economic anxieties of its partners, and the United States will resolve the current dysfunction of its government and accommodate itself to a more multipolar world.

Whatever the trajectory, Australia will be affected. America's complementarity with China may have ended, but Australia's has not.

The lucky country

The statistics about Australia's economic relations with China can seem eye-glazing.

Chinese demand accounts for 7 per cent of Australia's economy. Our two-way annual trade with China (A$230 billion) is greater than the sum of our trade with Japan, the United States and India combined. Even excluding minerals and energy, Australia's exports to China have risen by A$36.8 billion over the past decade, compared with A$9.86 billion for Japan and the United States combined.

The 1.3 million Chinese tourists who visited Australia in 2018 were responsible for one-quarter of all foreign tourist expenditure here. Our universities and schools host 205,000 Chinese students. These students' spending alone adds almost as much to our economy each year as our total trade with Great Britain.

The China–Australia Free Trade Agreement (ChAFTA), which entered into force in 2015, has dramatically boosted new areas of trade such as wine and dairy products.

Some commentators look at these figures and see an over-dependence on the Chinese market, opening us up to coercive pressures, such as recent efforts to slow down Australian exports of coal and barley. It's true that for any country – or any individual, for that matter – diversification is a sensible economic strategy. But the complementarity of the Australian and Chinese economies is broad and deep. From minerals and natural gas to horticultural products and sophisticated services, Australia is unusually well-placed to meet Chinese demand. Our exporters can, and should, look elsewhere, but no other potential partner – none – can offer Australia the scale and certainty of the Chinese market.

Investment is a more volatile measure of economic engagement with China. Aggregate Chinese investment in Australia nearly tripled between 2014 and 2016, when it reached a peak of A$15.8 billion, but it has since fallen by almost half each year. The Australian National University's Chinese Investment in Australia (CHIIA) database shows that Chinese investment in Australia has declined faster than the fall in its overall foreign investment.

It is legitimate and important for Australia to determine the sources of foreign investment in areas relevant to our national security. China does the same. But to develop a great continent we need continuing inflows of capital, and China will be an important source.

We can't assume that the economic relationship with China will continue to grow forever. The quality, price and reliability of

Australian products gives China plenty of reasons to stick with us, but as it shifts its engine of growth from investment to domestic consumption, and adjusts to the effects of climate change, some of the demand for Australian resources may fall. Services exports such as education and tourism will inevitably encounter new competition from domestic Chinese sources and eager international suppliers.

Australia's relationship with China extends well beyond our shared economic interests. China is a permanent member of the UN Security Council, and a leading member of the G20, APEC and the East Asia Summit. If we are to have any chance of influencing the outcome of regional or global issues of importance to us, ranging from climate change and the future of Antarctica to the control of lethal autonomous weapons, we will have to engage with China.

Reports of Chinese interference in Australia's domestic affairs are beginning to affect public opinion

A question of values

Our interests in China are clear enough, but what about our values, those beliefs fundamental to the way we define ourselves, whether as individuals or nations? Most of the discussion about values in relation to Australia and China focuses on those embedded in our political systems. Australia's liberal democracy, protecting individual rights and free speech under the rule of law, is very different from the authoritarian structure of a communist party-state, run along Leninist principles, in which the right to challenge the fundamental underpinnings of the system does not exist. These differences matter, in part because they affect the level of trust between our two nations.

But in international relations, values are seldom the sole determinant of government actions. They have to be weighed against interests, which often have a moral value of their own. A strong economy, for example, provides us with more opportunities to build a just society.

And values cannot be disentangled from the arena of power. China's capacity to assert its values and influence others is the reason values feature so much more prominently in our relationship with Beijing than with Vietnam, another authoritarian communist state.

But China is by no means unique. The world of liberal democracies is shrinking. The independent watchdog Freedom House has recorded thirteen years of consecutive decline in political rights and civil liberties. Of all the countries in the East Asia Summit, only Australia and New Zealand rate as full democracies in The Economist Intelligence Unit's annual democracy survey. Many governments with which Australia deals closely, from Vietnam and Thailand to the UAE, have values different from ours. If Australia did not engage with such countries, our influence in the world would be minimal.

China's presence in Australia

For a long time, according to the Lowy Institute's annual survey of Australian views of the world, China was seen more as an opportunity than a threat. Yet in 2019, a noticeable shift took place. Measures of trust and warmth plummeted. The number of Australians who trusted China "a great deal" or "somewhat" fell by 20 points in just a year, to 32 per cent. Nearly three-quarters of Australians now think that Australia is too economically dependent on China. Seventy-seven per cent (compared with 66 per cent in 2015) think Australia should "do more to resist China's military actions in our region, even if this affects our economic relationship".

Clearly, the widespread reports of Chinese interference in Australia's domestic affairs are beginning to affect public opinion. Stories of PRC pressure on individuals and their families in the Chinese-Australian community have heightened concern.

Unlike our relatively narrow-focus partnership with Japan, Australia's relationship with China involves a strong migrant community and increasing engagement from the Chinese government.

The Chinese-Australian community (those identifying as ethnically Chinese) includes descendants of those who arrived before and during the gold rushes of the nineteenth century; migrants from Chinese communities in Singapore, Malaysia and Vietnam; the 40,000 who stayed after Tiananmen; and waves of arrivals from Hong Kong, Taiwan and, more recently, the mainland. Since 2011, PRC citizens have been Australia's second-largest source, after Indians, of new migrants. Around the same number of Australians were born in China as in New Zealand. Some 900,000 of us speak Mandarin, Cantonese or another dialect at home.

Chinese-Australians now form significant minorities in several federal parliamentary seats. In 2019, the seat of Chisholm saw the first political contest in which the candidates of the two major parties were both of Chinese heritage (one from Hong Kong, the other from Taiwan). Research data suggests that Chinese-Australians split their voting preferences between parties in patterns very similar to other Australians.

Although the community features some fierce opponents of the policies of the Chinese government as well as staunch defenders, many Chinese-Australians are afraid of being labelled pro-PRC or having their loyalties to Australia called into question. Sinophobia is a clear memory for some who have come from South-East Asia. Some Australians with a Chinese family background, such as Penny Wong, have risen to the top of their professions, but there is still low representation of Chinese-Australians, and Asian-Australians generally, on ASX 200 boards, and in the judiciary and the public service. Anecdotal evidence suggests that some Chinese-Australians are self-selecting out of national security jobs in Canberra because of fears they would not be trusted to hold senior positions.

The Chinese government has always been concerned about the activities of groups in Australia such as Falun Gong or Tibet activists, which challenge the CCP's legitimacy. But its engagement with both Chinese-Australians and the broader community has expanded. In part, this is the legitimate work of any government trying to influence other states through soft power and diplomacy.

Confucius Institutes, paid newspaper supplements, dialogues with think tanks, cultural performances and government-sponsored visits for opinion leaders all fall into that category.

Some of the claims about Chinese interference in Australia are inflated. Foreign donations to our political parties have never been substantial and are now banned. Allegations of interference in universities boil down to a few incidents that seem to have been resolved appropriately. Australians who speak Mandarin seem perfectly able to recognise propaganda when they see it in local Chinese-language publications or online.

We can't know whether China will continue to grow or if deep social and economic problems lie ahead

Even so, evidence has mounted of intrusive interventions by China, including state-sponsored cyberattacks; intimidation of dissidents; control of students, including through their families; and efforts to shape covertly the positions of influential Australians. These are important matters. Protecting the integrity of our democratic institutions is a key responsibility of our government.

It is important to know where to draw the line. Australia is a democracy. If Australians want to argue that our government should support the reunification of Taiwan with China, or Chinese claims in the South China Sea (or oppose the use of the name Macedonia by a country that is not Greece, or encourage the independence of West Papua from Indonesia, or resist the idea of a two-state solution in Israel), they are welcome to do so. But we can and should hold the Chinese government to account over illicit activities. Whenever actions by Australian citizens or residents, or by foreign governments or their agents, slip into espionage, subversion or illegal interference, we have appropriate ways of dealing with them, including through non-discriminatory legislation, maximum transparency, community education, and well-resourced and managed security and police agencies.

Out in the cold

This has been a troubled period for relations between Australia and China.

The reasons for this are not found in Australia's official policy position towards China. All Australian prime ministers since John Howard have explained that stance in some variation of these words by Malcolm Turnbull, spoken in June 2018: "China will play a larger role in shaping the region. It is natural that Beijing will seek strategic influence to match its economic weight, but we want to see China build a leadership role it desires in a way which strengthens the regional order that has served us all so well."

There is a lot packed into that final phrase, but it's a solid foundation.

Certainly, decisions such as the effective ban on Chinese vendors in the 5G telecommunications system and our reluctance to sign up to the Belt and Road Initiative have upset China. A strong response was always likely. But the damage to the relationship has been magnified by the way Australian policymakers have explained and implemented those decisions.

Turnbull appropriated the purported words of Mao Zedong in saying that Australia had "stood up" to China, thereby framing a completely defensible policy directed against foreign interference in specifically Chinese terms. A government minister criticised China for building "roads to nowhere" in the South Pacific, simultaneously insulting Beijing and our Pacific neighbours. The 5G decision was trumpeted in press background as Australia's leadership of a "Five Eyes" campaign to move the world away from Chinese technology. Some media reports and commentary drew on the fevered language of "silent invasions" of "citizen spies" from China, and "multi-spectrum" and "grey zone" threats. The churn in Australia's leadership, and displays of a hard line towards China for other political purposes, also didn't help.

Chinese officials sometimes find it tactically useful to put Australia in its place by portraying us as a minor factotum dancing to America's tune. But in this case, the bragging about our role in the global pushback against Chinese power gave them an easier ride. Chinese displeasure with all these developments came in unmistakable terms. Visits from ministers, and even officials, have been difficult to arrange, and our diplomats in Beijing have found doors closed to them. No progress has been made in reviewing and expanding our free trade agreement. Overall trade volume has increased, but some exports, such as coal, have been slowed down or subjected to additional inspections.

This paralysis is not inevitable, even in a relationship that will always include elements of disagreement. We can do better.

How to handle China

To manage our relationship with one of the two countries that will do most to shape Australia's future, we have to be clear about our goals with China, consistent in the way we pursue them, calm in the face of some of the wilder claims about Beijing's actions and confident in our values.

We can't know whether China will continue to grow or if deep social and economic problems lie ahead. Its future leaders may be far-sighted statesmen (stateswomen are less likely) or dangerous risk-takers. We've seen examples of both in the past seventy years alone.

But our uncertainty doesn't change the fact that there is no Australian future – sunlit or shadowed – in which China will not be central. Avoiding tension with Beijing is not in itself a goal, but we do need to understand China in all its complexity and to engage with it as it is. The Chinese political system may be authoritarian, but individuals, institutions and interest groups contend within it. We have a far better chance of developing effective policies to respond to Chinese actions if we grasp how those dynamics affect government decisions.

We are not alone as we try to navigate the new world. We must work with others to build a region in which all countries can be heard and agreed rules are followed. But Australia's interests are national and particular: this is not a relationship we can outsource.

There will always be sound national security reasons to protect areas of our economy or advanced research. We can't engage blindly with China, without considering the risks and consequences. For example, our universities need to understand the links between scholarship and its practical outcomes. But it would be hard to think of a more damaging strategy than to cut ourselves off from engagement with one of the two most important global centres of international research. The rules we devise to protect ourselves should always follow the maxim "small yards with high walls".

We need to be calm in the face of hyperventilation about China

Our current national resources for dealing with China are hardly up to the task. We have few political leaders and officials with meaningful experience in China. Our government decision-making processes are not good enough at integrating economic and security interests. At our universities, we lack serious expertise on contemporary China and its elite politics. It's a reasonable guess that only about 130 Australians of non-Chinese background can conduct business in Chinese at the highest level of professionalism. We have not properly engaged Chinese-Australians in all their diversity in the national debate about China.

The Morrison government recently established a National Foundation for Australia–China Relations to promote ties in areas ranging from agriculture and health to education and the arts. It is a welcome initiative, but its total expenditure is A$44 million over five years. In contrast, we have had a lively national debate about the size of Australian defence spending and the structure of our military force, largely precipitated by China's rise. Is the current A$40 billion a year enough? Or do we need to spend A$70 billion?

Australians are frequently asked to think about China through particular prisms. The "China question" is often framed in the seductive language of grand strategy, with its Thucydides traps and Munich metaphors, a great power game of global significance in which Australia is a minor player. In other quarters, China is shaped primarily as a domestic security threat, an enemy within, stealthily working away at white-anting our democracy. In parts of the business community, the straight transactional benefits of easy sales into the Chinese market trump all else.

None of these perspectives can fully encompass the task at hand. Luckily, we have another way of approaching China. That is through the often disregarded (disdained in some quarters) work of foreign policy. Foreign policy is not diplomacy – that's the operating system underpinning it – and it is not the responsibility of a single government department. It is the daily business of engagement, negotiation, action and reaction across the span of government activities, bilateral and multilateral, by which our government advances our interests with China and protects our values. It is the part of statecraft whose purpose is the slow, grinding job of managing differences between states in the international system; the arduous task of constructing, brick by brick, the foundation of a stable international order.

Foreign policy helps us weigh and balance our interests and values by thinking about them together as common national stakes we have in the relationship with China. How far, for example, should we go in criticising China on human rights issues? For Australia, non-interference in the internal affairs of another country does not mean refraining from comment on decisions taken by other governments.

Sometimes we cannot remain silent. We will want to take action or place our views firmly on the public record. But at other times, to the frustration of advocacy groups, quiet diplomacy and avoiding a loss of face really is the best long-term way of resolving an issue. In certain situations, we will, properly, measure the likely impact of our response against the other stakes we have in the relationship – economic opportunities, security interests, promoting a stable international order – and act accordingly.

We need to be calm in the face of some of the hyperventilation and wilder claims about China. The PRC has become more authoritarian and hostile to dissent in recent years, but it is not the Orwellian dystopia portrayed in some Western commentary. Beijing is not taking over the developing world through debt-trap diplomacy. Its influence in the South Pacific is growing, but it is not supplanting Australian aid. It is not remotely surprising that, as a "national security source" breathlessly told an Australian journalist recently, China's spy satellites would "almost certainly" be monitoring Australia–US naval exercises off the Queensland coast. China's use of economic coercion to advance its interests (as with its efforts to force South Korea to abandon the installation of a US ballistic-missile defence system) has been largely unsuccessful so far. As we saw in the way it shifted its positions on the structure of the AIIB and the Belt and Road Initiative, China, like all states, responds to the reactions of others.

Finally, we need confidence in ourselves and our values. History hasn't ended. If, as I believe and Australia's leaders affirm, individual freedom, representative systems and strong civil society organisations deliver better outcomes over time, then either China will discover these things for itself – in its own way and in line with its own historical experience and cultural values – or its capacity to grow and to influence others will be self-limiting.

The Middle Kingdom is not returning. In Professor Nick Bisley's useful distinction, the broader Indo-Pacific is likely to be China-centred but not Sino-centric. In other words, China will be the most powerful state in the region, but not unchallenged. There will be no contemporary version of the Qing dynasty tributary system. China's Asian neighbours – Japan, India, Indonesia – are too powerful and too deeply familiar with China for that to happen. The United States may no longer be the regional hegemon but, Donald Trump notwithstanding, it will retain, in its own right and in concert with others, a powerful capacity to balance and influence outcomes in East Asia.

The United States is not the only country whose relative power is slipping. In the early 1990s, the Australian economy was larger than those of all the other ASEAN countries combined. By some measures,

Indonesia's economy alone is now nearly three times the size of Australia's. That doesn't mean absolute decline, but it does mean we will have to work harder to assert our national influence.

The comforting familiarity of the post–World War II era has ended and the strangeness of our international environment, including China's centrality, is here to stay. Learning how to adjust to the strangeness and operate effectively within it is this generation's great national test. ▨

HIGH PRICE

Inside the Chinese
student boom

Margaret Simons

International education is one of Australia's largest export industries, coming in behind coal, iron ore and now the natural gas industry. But there is a dissonance here – a contradiction.

There is surely a difference between digging, extracting and shipping out the earth's resources, and bringing in hundreds of thousands of young people, all in search of self-improvement, a leg up in the job market back home, a better life in Australia, or all three. Mining exports are relatively simple. Young people are complicated.

The education of international students, including their tuition fees and the money they spend on accommodation, food and other living expenses, brings in an estimated A$35.2 billion, or 8 per cent of total exports. It's a massive business.

Chinese students represent about one-third of the students who come to Australia, but a larger proportion of the dollars – because they gravitate to the prestige of Australia's top universities, where the fees are higher. They have already transformed the campuses and our cities. Step into a lift at any leading Australian university and you are as likely to hear Mandarin spoken as English. Visit the café strips nearby and drink bubble tea, a sweet tapioca-bead drink. It was almost unheard of in Australia fifteen years ago; now it is everywhere. So are cheap and good noodles. International students are also one of the main drivers of the high-rise micro apartment trend in our inner cities.

Such changes, though, are superficial. They could be reversed quickly. Underlying them are bigger shifts in the way this country works. Chief among these is the interaction between immigration policy and education. We are selling not only degrees and qualifications, but also access to the Australian labour market and insights into our way of life. The boom in international students is part of a fundamental change in Australian immigration – from an entirely controlled, capped system of permanent migration to an intake that includes a largely uncapped intake of temporary migrants. These temporary migrants include backpackers and overseas workers, but students make up a large cohort and are driving the increase. They are likely to stay longer – a significant proportion gain permanent residency.

So, almost without public controversy, or even public awareness, universities rather than the federal government are determining, to quote former prime minister John Howard, a large proportion of "who comes to this country and the circumstances in which they come".

The students are not the same as truckloads of ore. They are of course changed by their Australian education, as we would hope. But perhaps they are not changed as much as they change us.

The rankings cycle

Chinese students have altered the dynamics of our top universities, which are now largely dependent on this single market – particularly to foster the research effort that has propelled them up the world rankings.

International rankings of tertiary institutions – the Times Higher Education list and the Shanghai Jiao Tong list are probably the best known – are increasingly important to universities. They are, rightly or wrongly, taken as markers of success. They are also what draw prestige-conscious students, such as the Chinese. Those rankings are mostly determined by research, as measured by publication in prestigious international journals.

It's one of the unfailing rules of human institutions that if you introduce a measurement, the system changes to meet it, like the leaves of a plant turning to face the sun. So it is that the research output the international rankings measure grows lush at universities, and those sides of academia not rewarded can dwindle in the shade. One of those things can be teaching. Another is the kind of industry-connected research that can be useful, but doesn't reach the international journals.

The students lured to our leading universities may never encounter the academics behind the research that attracted the ranking.

Instead, they are often taught by sessional staff and those on short-term contracts. According to the National Tertiary Education Union, only one-third of Australian university staff have secure employment, or tenure. Forty-three per cent are casuals – their contracts end at the end of each semester. Twenty-two per cent are on fixed-term contracts, typically between one and two years in length. So, universities have become big employers, but not particularly good employers.

Meanwhile, according to researcher Andrew Norton, who was until recently based at the Grattan Institute, major universities are pumping out more research, leading to rising rankings, leading to more international students, who subsidise more research.

Chinese students make up 60 per cent of all foreign student enrolments

To Norton, the increasing casualisation of the academic workforce is a de-facto risk management strategy. If the boom in international students stopped, universities could downsize much more easily. But the same equation applies: less teaching, less research, a lower position in the rankings.

The money from international students has allowed our universities to do well through a period in which government funding, for both teaching and research, has been cut. It is hardly reasonable to expect them to turn the business away. Yet they are living through a boom. Perhaps the landing will be hard, perhaps it will be soft. What are our best universities doing to manage the risk? What's the plan for the future? It's not easy to get satisfactory answers.

China and prestige

The export industry for international education involves five sectors, including school and vocational education and training. Higher education – universities – is by far the largest sector. Chinese students are the largest cohort: 30 per cent of the 595,363 international students currently in Australia. The next largest cohorts are from India, at 15 per cent; Nepal, at 7 per cent; and Vietnam and Malaysia, at 4 per cent each.

As a group, the Chinese often behave differently from students of other nationalities. Most are only children, the legacy of China's one-child policy. They are the focus of the ambitions and financial resources of both parents and two sets of grandparents. For these families, the prestige bestowed by a top university is important. Meanwhile, students from India and the other developing countries are more likely to be from larger, poorer families. They generally attend vocational colleges and second-tier universities, where the fees are lower, and many hope to use their time in Australia as a stepping-stone to permanent residency and, eventually, citizenship.

The story of Chinese students is mainly about Australia's top institutions of research and higher learning – the so-called Group of Eight (Go8). They are the Australian National University, Monash

University, the University of Melbourne, the University of New South Wales, the University of Queensland, the University of Sydney, the University of Western Australia and the University of Adelaide. Seven are ranked in the top 100 in the world, and all are in the top 150. Since the Chinese student boom began, most of them have risen in those rankings. These universities charge around A$40,000 a year for courses, compared to around A$25,000 a year by the non-Go8 universities.

At the Go8, Chinese students make up 60 per cent of all foreign student enrolments. According to analysis published earlier this year in the *Journal of Higher Education Policy and Management*, the Go8 now earn more from Chinese students than they do from the Commonwealth Grant Scheme, the basic teaching grant that the government pays for the education of domestic students. In 2017, 43 per cent of commencing students at the Australian National University and the University of Sydney were from overseas, as well as 40 per cent of commencing students at Monash. In 2012, it was 23 per cent at the University of Sydney and 24 per cent at Monash. Similar rapid rises have occurred at most Go8 universities.

Australia is the most common destination for students from China after the United States, and the third-largest player in the international student market, after the United States and the United Kingdom. The market in Australia is segmented, with universities tending to be dominated by particular ethnic groups. Andrew Norton notes that this increases the risk for individual institutions.

A downturn in the flow of students from Vietnam, for example, would have a significant impact at a university such as Melbourne's RMIT, but leave others relatively untouched. A downturn in students from China would hit the Go8 very hard indeed.

The Chinese student experience

Time to declare my position in this story. I work at Monash University, one of the Go8, teaching journalism subjects. Before that, I headed the Master of Journalism at another Go8 member, the University of Melbourne. I teach Chinese students. The journalism-focused subjects don't draw these students in large numbers. Partly, this is because a Western-oriented journalism education is of limited use in China. Partly it is because we demand higher English language skills. But I have also taught into broader media and communications degrees, where it is common for lectures to contain up to 80 per cent Chinese students.

Chinese students have been among my best and worst pupils. The obvious differences – English language capabilities chief among them – obscure the many ways in which they mirror any other cohort. Some students are diligent; others are clearly satisfying parental ambitions rather than pursuing their own. They are often away from parental control and day-to-day support for the first time, with all that implies for fun, personal growth and stress.

In practical journalism assignments, Chinese students naturally gravitate to reporting on their own community. So it is that I have learned, from them, about students who support themselves by smuggling illicit tobacco from China to Australia. I have seen many reports about the Daigou – students and others who buy goods for customers back home concerned about food safety and purity.

My top student last year was Chinese. I will call her Mary, rather than using her real name, for reasons that will become clear. She completed, to high distinction standard, an investigative report on the contract cheating business.

Websites that sell essays are marketed to Chinese students in English language countries worldwide. My student interviewed some of those who write the essays. They charge $150 per 1000 words for an assignment

Australian universities are depriving both their international customers and domestic students

designed to attract a pass mark, or more for a credit or a distinction. This is not plagiarism. These are real, original assignments – just not written by the enrolled student. I'd be lying if I said I was confident in spotting them when they cross my desk.

Thanks to Mary's work, I know that one of the biggest agencies, Meeloun Education, claims to have over 450 writers, more than half with master's degrees from outside China. They spruik that they can handle assignments in all the major Australian universities, specifically mentioning the University of Sydney, the University of Melbourne, the University of Adelaide and Monash University.

On the strength of this work, Mary got an internship at the Australian Broadcasting Corporation, which has since published its own stories on the contract cheating business. There is now legislation planned to outlaw these websites. Meanwhile, Mary has graduated and secured work helping Australian journalists who are investigating Chinese influence in Australia. She never gets a byline – that would be dangerous – and she doesn't tell her Chinese friends what she is doing.

I meet Mary in Federation Square, central Melbourne, after asking if she will talk to me for this article. She is thrilled. She tells me she has mentioned our meeting to her mother. Such contact is rare enough to be significant news. This, she says, is the hardest thing for Chinese students. Australians are friendly to them on a superficial basis, but "this notion of personal space, that is very strange and very hard". Many Chinese students find it hard to penetrate, or even understand, the reserve that surrounds our intimate lives. How can we be so affable, yet back away so fast when a Chinese student responds with an expectation of greater intimacy?

Mary is unusual. Her encounters with Australian journalists mean she absorbs local news and views, and her English is flawless. Yet she still struggles to engage with Australians. Most of her Chinese student friends, meanwhile, move through Australian society in a bubble. They speak English only in class. They consume little Australian media, instead relying heavily on Chinese language social media news services, targeted to Chinese students in Australia.

Associate professor Fran Martin at the University of Melbourne has been conducting a five-year study of Chinese international students. Her subjects are all women – partly due to her research speciality in gender studies, but also because 60 per cent of all Chinese students overseas are female. This imbalance is even more striking given that women comprise fewer than 50 per cent of the Chinese population, thanks to a skewed birth ratio under the one-child policy.

Martin found that the failure to make Australian friends is a major disappointment for Chinese students. Making friends from other countries is one of their main motivations for coming to Australia. They blame their failure on poor English language skills, but Martin sees this as a symptom, not a cause. Australian universities aren't doing enough to provide them with the experience they seek. The best way to learn a language is to use it – and Chinese students don't get those opportunities. She tells me, "It's an indictment on the universities that they don't do more to break up the cliques, to force interaction." Teaching staff aren't trained in the kind of cross-cultural skills needed. They should be doing more to encourage student interaction, she says, and this in turn would help international students improve their English. By failing to do this, Australian universities are depriving both their international customers and the domestic students, who could benefit from such interaction. Despite the numbers of international students, we are not running a genuinely international system of education.

Professor Sue Elliott, deputy vice-chancellor at Monash University, told me that universities are investing in support such as English language assistance and Mandarin-speaking mental health services. How much of the revenue raised by Chinese students is spent on such services? I could not find a single university that releases those figures, though all of those I spoke to nominate the failure to integrate Chinese students as a major risk to the goose that lays those golden eggs.

The experience of being in Australia changes female Chinese students, says Martin, but perhaps not in the ways we might expect. The women return home with a greater sense of independence and are more likely to resist state and family pressure to marry early and have children. But when asked if this is because of their contact with Australian values, they are likely to dismiss the idea. Rather, it was the experience of being away from family that formed them, together with an awareness of the time and money spent on their education.

Australian politics can also be puzzling for Chinese students. Living in the city, they see every demonstration that brings the streets to a halt. Martin says many are intrigued: why are people bothering? When it is explained that enough public attention might change votes, and that might change the government, they understand – but are unlikely to change their view.

This mirrors my experiences in the classroom. In my subjects, Chinese students are often openly critical of their own government, but when China is criticised by others, they can be defensive. Even the journalism students, who crave more media freedom at home, will argue that China's large population and many challenges necessitate strong party rule. It is rare for a student from China to advocate a Western system of media freedom. And most resent the way in which the Australian media depicts China – and their presence on campus – as a threat.

In 2017, then foreign minister Julie Bishop made a statement warning Chinese students to respect freedom of speech at Australian universities amid growing unease over Beijing's alleged influence on campuses. Martin says most of her subjects weren't aware of the statement until it was picked up by Chinese language social media. Then, they were "outraged – very offended".

For Chinese students, it is comparatively easy to get into a top Australian university for graduate study

It has been one of the tropes, this allegation that Chinese students attempt to suppress freedom of speech. Sometimes they are accused of trying to close down debate in lectures. The same couple of anecdotes tend to get recycled – and helped to provoke a recent government review of freedom of speech on campus, conducted by former High Court chief justice Robert French, which found no evidence of a systemic problem.

Yet Fran Martin, Sue Elliott and Mary all told me they had never seen any evidence that Chinese students were either threatened or threatening when it came to freedom of speech. I had never seen it myself, nor had any of the colleagues I asked about this. Then, in the week after I conducted interviews for this essay, there were the reports of pro–Hong Kong democracy protesters on campuses being harassed and attacked. This made Martin reconsider her earlier statement, but "it's a very tiny minority of Chinese students who are involved in such incidents".

Mary does not rule out that there may be Chinese spies on campus, watching their fellow students, including people like her who express independent views in class. She would speak freely in a class where she knew the individuals, she said, but would be more careful in an open forum. On the other hand, she had seen students question lecturers in class, including on topics to do with China – but they were taking part in class discussions, not trying to close them down. And, she asked, wasn't that an example of freedom of speech? Wasn't that something we encouraged? Or were only certain kinds of free speech encouraged?

Meanwhile, Mary has asked the Australian journalists she works with whether they feel they are objective about China. Why do they always cast it as a threat? They tell her they are just writing the facts.

"What do you think?" I ask.

She shrugs and smiles. "I am still trying to find out that answer," she says. She is also trying to work out which country's media to trust.

"Your life is very complicated," I say to Mary, and she agrees.

The language problem

For Chinese students, it is comparatively easy to get into a top Australian university for graduate study. Apart from the English language test, there are no entrance exams, unlike the gruelling selection system in China. Applicants for entry to Australian universities are assessed entirely on the scores from their undergraduate degree. For many, it comes as a shock to discover that, despite having paid top dollar, there is no guarantee they won't fail. In China, getting in is hard, but once accepted, graduating is virtually guaranteed. Failed assignments can always be resubmitted. Exams can be re-sat.

The other issue is English language standards.

This is the most frequent cause of discussion, and complaint, in the staffrooms of universities. Too often, Chinese students clearly lack the English language skills to profit from their education. And this, of course, causes the pressures that underlie the contract cheating business.

Andrew Norton says it is common knowledge among everyone who teaches Chinese students that there is a problem with English language skills, but it is one of the most profound areas of lack of data. "Is it 20 per cent, 30 per cent, 40 per cent or 90 per cent of students?" he says. "We just don't have the data." Why not? He suggests it is because nobody wants to know the answer. "The government and the unis and the industry as a whole are so passionately committed to this business and to the money that it brings in. That is stopping critical analysis of what's really going on."

This is just one example of a lack of data in the international education business. Sometimes, one suspects it is because nobody has an interest in filling the gaps. It is hard to imagine any other export business that would tolerate such a deficiency of key information.

The English language test score most commonly used in admission applications is the International English Language Testing System (IELTS). The IELTS organisation recommends an entry score of at least seven – the highest score is nine – for linguistically demanding courses such as those in the arts and humanities. All Australian universities allow students into humanities degrees on a score of 6.5.

I had one student who made the mistake of studying a single journalism practice subject as an elective in her communications degree. She can't have known that we required students to complete writing exercises in class to deadline – an attempt to replicate newsroom pressures.

It quickly became clear that she couldn't write a word of English. I asked the university admissions team to check her IELTS score. We found that the photo of the student who had sat the IELTS test back in China was not the student now attending class. This young woman was eventually thrown out of the university for fraud – a harsh but correct result. But I often think of her, and what her presence meant. Until enrolling in my journalism subject, she had been passing most of her essay-based subjects with a high pass or a credit. Can we be sure that if she had avoided journalism, she wouldn't have passed the entire degree?

Against isolated cases like this, there are many Chinese students who work hard to overcome language difficulties. And there are many stories of alumni who have gone on to stellar careers, aided by their Australian degree.

There is no doubt that large numbers of Chinese students in a class changes the way you teach. At the trivial level, I speak more slowly and avoid the use of idiom. I put more words on the Power-Points and make greater use of handouts. Because Chinese students are reluctant to speak in class, I design exercises where they can't get out of it.

Other techniques I avoid, but have heard of, include setting group assignments, and pairing the strongest domestic

Ask universities about risk, and you can get a prickly response

with the weakest international students. I am dubious about the claimed educational benefits. It can be used to get the whole cohort through, while hoping that everyone learns something along the way.

As for soft marking, I don't doubt that it happens – but it can be subjective. In journalism, for example, we set high language requirements for our domestic students, deducting marks for errors of grammar and punctuation. This is necessary to fit graduates for the local media industry. Is it soft marking or mere common sense to emphasise, in the marking of international students, their nose for news, their grasp of structure, their ideas and critical thinking, and pass over grammatical errors? After all, they will be returning home to practise. These are the decisions university staff make, largely on their own and without guidance from faculty.

The minister for education, Dan Tehan, recently wrote to the Tertiary Education Quality and Standards Agency – responsible for regulating standards at our institutions of higher learning – to ask about English language requirements. TEQSA wrote back describing at length the mechanisms that apply and concluded "there is little evidence to suggest that there is a systemic failure regarding compliance with English language entry requirements". One can only think they haven't been in class.

Norton believes that if the government, or universities, were concerned to better manage both the risk and the growth of the international student market, lifting English language skills would be the most effective way to do it. It would cause a soft slide in the numbers, but result in more satisfaction among the students, both domestic and international. And, for those who use a student visa as a path to long-term residency in Australia, it would mean they had a better chance of making their way.

Ask the representatives of universities about risk, and you can get a prickly response. The chief executive of Universities Australia, Catriona Jackson, says she is puzzled – even a little affronted – that discussion of what should be regarded as a success story always turns to risk. She says the current boom is the legacy of a decision made by universities fifty years ago to develop the international education market, and this has been boosted by China's rise. "This has been a long, slow build done very consciously by very sophisticated organisations that don't just open the doors in the last two minutes but have thought about this really carefully."

And of course, the problems should not obscure the reality that international education is a success story. But Jackson's is a sunny view of a history that is in fact very mixed. Although, to be fair, most of the missteps have been made by government rather than by universities.

The accidental boom

In the 1950s, Australia offered education to those in Asia-Pacific countries under the Colombo Plan as a means of tempering racism and winning the battle of hearts and minds during the Cold War. Thousands of students from Asia were sponsored to study or train in Australia. The result was one of the happiest chapters in the history of our relations with the region. Most of the students returned to their home countries, many taking up leadership positions.

Immigration was an entirely separate area of policy from education. The emphasis was on building Australia through permanent migration, both making and expecting a long-term commitment.

In 1996, under the Howard government, that changed. Australia entered the highly competitive business of trying to attract the best migrants. Extra points were awarded to applicants who had an Australian educational qualification. This created an incentive for prospective migrants to enter as students. As a result, international student numbers boomed. By 2007, when Howard lost power, Australia was taking 97,000 skilled migrants a year, 40 per cent of whom were already in Australia – most having entered as international students.

The government listed occupational skills said to be in demand, which attracted extra points. Dodgy colleges sprang up. Never before had there been so many opportunities to study cooking, hairdressing and hospitality in Australia, and never before had so many young people from overseas apparently wanted to learn to be cooks, hairdressers and waiters. Total international students in all sectors reached 632,000 in 2009 – phenomenal growth of 17 per cent on the previous year. But then came the crash.

After the global financial crisis, the Rudd government introduced a new system, with priority given to migrants sponsored by employers. The minister for immigration, Chris Evans, said, "A student visa is just that: a visa to study … Australia's migration program is not and should not be determined by the courses studied by international students." This was in complete contradiction to most of the previous fifteen years of policy settings – and it didn't last.

The changes caused the collapse of many of the dodgier colleges, but they also hit universities. The number of overseas student visas issued in higher education had peaked at 133,859 in 2008–09. In 2011–12, it dropped to 113,160.

It was a crisis, and the universities began to lobby government. By 2011, Canberra had made changes. The switch was meant to be to quality, and to directing students to reputable institutions that could be trusted to manage their share of the business. This coincided with China's rapidly increasing appetite for prestige international education and an increasing capacity to pay. In 2002, enrolments from China comprised 14 per cent of total international higher education enrolments. Today, it is over one-third.

One of Australia's competitive advantages in the international education market is that graduates can apply for a visa that allows them to work for two to four years after completing their qualification. Once, migrants applied from overseas and made their way through a tightly controlled government system. Today, half of permanent residency visas go

> **A complete halt in student migration is unlikely. Almost certain is a slow decline**

to people who are already in Australia. Temporary visa holders make up more than half of net overseas migration, and students are about one-third of that. For students, it is universities that set the entry standards – including English language skill level – and make the crucial decisions on who to take. As the Productivity Commission remarked, somewhat acidly, in a 2016 review of migration intake: "The purpose of immigration regulations is not to enhance the attractiveness of the international education services sector, and not all former international students possess the characteristics of the most desirable immigrants."

Yet the possibility of staying in Australia is generally acknowledged to be the main motivator for students from India, Nepal and the developing world, and a big competitive advantage for Australian higher education institutions.

Martin says Chinese students are not necessarily focused on migration but do aspire to international professional mobility – to the option of living and working overseas. Bob Birrell, head of the Australian Population Research Institute, estimates that about 80 per cent of Chinese students return home on graduation, based on Chinese government figures. But that still leaves us with a cohort of long-term Chinese and other residents who lack rights, cannot vote – including for policies that directly affect them – and are not asked to make the kinds of commitments we expect of citizens.

Mary, now on a temporary graduation visa, is a good example. She hopes to stay in Australia. Partly it is because of the clean air. Partly it is because of our better welfare system. Her mother also worries that there will be problems in China – an economic collapse or a political purge. A child in Australia would be a hedge against such risks.

There is also the increased freedom of speech. But there is a contradiction here. While Mary is no passive consumer of her country's propaganda, nor is she becoming more wedded to an Australian identity. Her generation, she says, is proud that China is growing in influence and power. Migration to the West is seen as part of China's rise, the taking of its place as an international power. It's an attitude full of contradictions – an attraction to Australia because it offers a better life, but also a cleaving to the home country and its strategic priorities.

"We might criticise our government and President Xi Jinping. But when we are in Australia and we hear other people criticise, naturally we want to defend," says Mary. She and her friends aspire to the option of life in Australia but "unlike the Greeks or the Italians, we see ourselves as different. We will always be *Chinese* Australians."

Risky business?

So, what would happen to our best universities if the flow of Chinese students slackened? When and how will the boom end?

One of the main risks is geopolitics: the possibility that deteriorating ties between Australia and China will lead to the government shutting off or slowing the flow of students.

Sue Elliott says the sector is well aware that China could simply turn off the tap. She thinks it unlikely, but it would be devastating. Building programs would be cut, courses would have to be reviewed for viability, and the universities' research efforts would suffer.

The effects would flow out into the city. The Real Estate Institute of Australia was unable to provide figures on the impact of a drop in student numbers on the apartment market, but we can all imagine the fallout. The centres of our cities would thin out, the impact spreading through to the wider economy.

Some think the boom will continue. University Australia's Catriona Jackson is upbeat. "The stat that always kills me is two-thirds of the world's middle class is going to be in Asia by 2030. Two thirds! ... And in China 20 per cent of the population will be middle-class by 2030. So I just find this discussion of decline quite strange."

Barring an international crisis, a complete halt in student migration is unlikely. Almost certain is a slow decline as Chinese universities improve. Australian governments have been cutting funding for universities, but China is investing hugely. The incentives for students to travel for education are reducing, and the Chinese government is increasingly likely to encourage its best and brightest to stay at home.

What about diversification? Elliott is frank about the difficulties. Other source countries are growing "quite strongly" but there is nothing that can match the Chinese numbers and capacity to pay. Barring a geopolitical crisis, she expects the business to continue solidly for the next ten to fifteen years. "I think there will still for that time be an esteem attached to an Australian or UK or US degree, and that will still be a market advantage."

The main risk to the business is its success. Chinese students invest big money and years of their lives seeking an international experience, and arrive to find classes full of their countrymen, and institutions altered, even distorted, by their presence.

We can only hope for a soft landing, and that a legacy of the boom will be increased mutual understanding with our trading partner, rather than imported cynicism on both sides.

The consequences

I gave a guest lecture recently to students visiting from a prestigious Chinese university. There was plenty of discussion afterwards, including about what these students had heard about China while in Australia. Their visit coincided with the thirtieth anniversary of the Tiananmen Square massacre – a banned topic in China. Some had watched the ABC's *Four Corners* special on the subject. They were also following the Australian news reports on the Hong Kong pro-democracy demonstrations.

One of the students argued that it was inevitable China would gradually become more democratic. Others thought this unlikely. One spoke up against Xi Jinping and his removal of presidential term limits. "We have a new emperor now," she said.

Australian economic, migration and education policies have become enmeshed without much strategic thought

None of these students seemed to fear speaking out in front of their fellows.

Finally, one of the women, who was perhaps eighteen years old, told me she had read on Chinese social media that the Hong Kong protesters had been encouraged and financed by hostile foreign powers, but she had seen no mention of this in the Australian media.

"Do you believe it?" I asked.

"I don't know what to believe," she said.

As she spoke, she looked, for a moment, as though she was in physical pain. Then she looked profoundly sad. The journalist in me thought, self-servingly, that this is the anguish of insufficient access to reliable information – that this is why journalism is important. The teacher in me, and perhaps the mother, worried about her obvious distress. What were we doing to her, and to all these young people, exposing them to so many contradictions, so much to process and think through, with no way and no licence to reach out and give a supporting hand when they return home?

It is arrogant to think we could be helpful if we could. More likely, we'd make it worse.

For these students, we send mixed messages. We have good intentions, sure – as well as a profit motive and a boom mentality. But add together the data gaps, the rush to get them in the door, the different kinds of exploitation we exercise on them, and they on us, and we don't have clean hands, or pure motives.

Australian economic, migration and education policies have become enmeshed without much evidence of clear strategic thought. Now it's hard to pull any thread without impacting on the whole garment.

So long as the business grows, the tensions and problems are hidden. But the boom almost certainly won't last.

It's nice to think that perhaps it is not too late to do better. The huge numbers of international students are unprecedented in the history of Australian tertiary education. We are educating swathes of the Chinese middle class at a time of geopolitical tension. There are such opportunities here, such important potential outcomes.

Academics could be trained in cross-cultural skills. Universities could invest more in welcoming student cohorts and supporting their integration with the domestic body. We could learn from our students, coming to better understand the Chinese point of view. Rather than bemoaning their impact on the way we teach, we could make a more genuine attempt to reach our students, to truly educate.

But all that would take investment, including by taxpayers, and wisdom. It would mean seeing foreign students not only as dollar signs, and education not only as a business – not comparable to coal and iron ore. It would mean being willing to seize the opportunity that resides in young people, in human engagement. Is it too late for this kind of strategic vision? ■

TRADE DEFICITS

How China could punish Australia

Richard McGregor

In July 2019, in a story applauding the construction of a new gas pipeline from Russia, Chinese newspaper *The Global Times* made sure to play up an additional benefit of the project. Not only would the pipeline bring more gas from Russia, the paper stated. It also meant that China could cut down on imports of liquified natural gas from Australia.

From the moment Australia's ties with Beijing began to sour, Chinese officials, scholars and commentators have pushed a similar menacing message. The state media, in its various manifestations, has consistently warned Australia that its China policy is "suicidal" for economic ties. Don't think you can "dig gold" in China, one scholar has said, while riding on America's coat-tails elsewhere. *The Global Times*, the Chinese Communist Party–owned tabloid that has long acted as Beijing's foreign policy bovver boy, is just one in a long line of outlets telling Australia not to bite the hand that feeds it.

The bigger China gets, the more willing it is to throw its weight around. Little wonder, then, that such threats have put the Australian government and business on edge about possible economic coercion from Beijing. Having staked their political credibility on ending years of budget deficits, prime minister Scott Morrison and treasurer Josh Frydenberg have a nervous eye on trade ties.

The budget is already primed for a windfall in corporate tax receipts, courtesy of sky-high iron ore prices, driven by strong steel production in China and supply disruptions in Brazil. There is no doubt a temptation to soft-pedal the politics of relations with China to ensure trade ties are not interrupted. Certainly, the idea that Australia is at Beijing's mercy on the economy is entrenched in the popular media. "If China decided to get narky with us," Channel 7's David Koch said to Morrison in an August 2019 interview, "we go into depression. It's as simple as that."

The immediate outlook for Australia's political relationship with China is not good. In any given week, the number of issues that are the focus of governmental dispute or popular sourness is astounding. Crown Casino and Chinese high rollers. Nasty, racially tinged spats between rival swimming stars. The South China Sea. Hong Kong, which spilled over into fights on Australian campuses. Controversy over Uyghurs with Australian passports or residency struggling to leave China. The hacking of Australian universities and the federal parliament. The blocking of ministerial visits. Canberra's treatment of Huawei, the Chinese telecommunications company. Gladys Liu.

Calls for an Australian military build-up in and around Darwin. Head-on competition in Papua New Guinea and the Pacific. The arrest of Chinese-Australian writer Yang Hengjun. If one issue involving China isn't dominating the news, another invariably is.

With the relationship in such disarray, the fear of Chinese economic coercion is entirely rational. In recent years, Beijing has used its growing economic weight to sanction numerous countries, most notably South Korea, which was hit in 2017 over its deployment of a US missile shield that Beijing said infringed on its sovereignty. Beijing restricted rare earths exports to Japan in 2010 after a territorial dispute flared up. The same year, Norwegian salmon imports were cut when a Chinese dissident was awarded the Nobel Peace Prize. The Philippines suffered in 2012 and 2016 when their territorial disputes with Beijing in the South China Sea reignited. Visits by the Dalai Lama have often been followed by cancellations of export orders.

China is not shy about advertising its muscle either. In recent months, Beijing has said that Canada will face "repercussions" if it bans Huawei from its new mobile phone network. Likewise, Turkey has been warned that "commercial and economic relations" will be damaged if Ankara keeps criticising the internment of Muslim Uyghurs in Xinjiang.

So far in Australia, however, the fevered debate about the threat of Chinese coercion has run far ahead of any action. Some Australian wine has been held up in Chinese ports. And, for much of 2019 Chinese importers of thermal coal have turned away or slowed the unloading of cargoes from Australia. In both cases, the Chinese actions carried a strong stench of politics, but they also involved other factors, such as difficulties in managing new customs rules for foreign wine and coal traders' attempts to take advantage of price fluctuations. Hugh White, a prominent commentator on security issues, has joked that many Australians began to panic about sanctions before Beijing "had even begun to clear its throat".

Certainly that was the case when the shipments from Treasury Wines were held up in Shanghai in early 2018. Top company executives bombarded then prime minister Malcolm Turnbull's office with phone calls demanding he intervene to get the wine off the docks. The company's chairman, Graham Kraehe, intoned gravely about regional geopolitics. "We can't rely on the US to be a big player in the Asia region," he said. The company's anxious musings turned out to be overly pessimistic. Since that hiccup, Treasury's sales into China have continued to grow.

The fevered debate about the threat of Chinese coercion has run far ahead of any action

Running in parallel to the debate on China's economic coercion have been increasing calls to find new export markets to reduce reliance on China. Australia should diversify its markets before China finds new sources of supplies. Or, as the old joke goes, we had better get our retaliation in first. Peter Varghese, in his 2018 report to government on strengthening ties with New Delhi, was explicit about the need for diversification and the value of India in that quest. "There is no other single market in the world that has more growth opportunities for Australia than India," wrote the former secretary of the Department of Foreign Affairs and Trade.

Not everyone thinks this approach will work. According to James Laurenceson and Michael Zhou of the Australia-China Relations Institute (ACRI), such prescriptions misunderstand why trade flourishes in the first place. Unlike security ties, trade is largely determined by market forces, a mix of economic complementarities and purchasing power, "not elected officials or bureaucrats sitting in Canberra".

The search for alternative markets is not unique to Australia. Canada even has a Minister for International Trade Diversification, in part aimed at weaning the country off an over-reliance on North America for business. But for now, in Australia, diversification seems good in theory but difficult in practice.

Whatever China has been up to, it hasn't hurt bilateral trade so far. In 2018, a year of seething tensions, when Beijing froze official contacts with Canberra and cold-shouldered Australian business, two-way trade went up year-on-year by more than 17 per cent, totalling A$193 billion, according to DFAT.

The continued strong growth in trade, substantially in Australia's favour, confirms a decade-long trend, which has seen China outperform all other markets for Australian exports by a large distance. According to ACRI's tabulation, exports to China have increased by A$78.5 billion over the past decade, nearly tripling in value.

By contrast, sales to Japan and the United States have been stagnant. Exports to India and Indonesia, two countries often touted as Australia's future, have risen by just A$5 billion. In June 2019, China took a record 40 per cent of all Australian exports.

But the politics of dealing with China means that the explosion in trade is often depicted as a vulnerability as much as a cause for national celebration. Chris Renwick, who as a Rio Tinto lawyer wrote the first contract for iron ore shipments to China in 1970, two years before the establishment of diplomatic ties, remembers that Chinese buyers used to ask for a discount in the early days, because, they said, they couldn't compete with the Japanese. The first sale of iron ore to China was considered a commercial coup at the time. Until then, China had only imported iron ore from North Korea. Now North Korea is an afterthought and Japan is a sideshow. It is Chinese demand that drives the market. Renwick, who went on to head Rio's iron ore operations, reflects the view of many business leaders these days when he says the tables have been turned in bilateral economic relations. The power balance today runs in China's favour. "They needed us then," he said. "Now they believe that we need them."

China's long memory

For all the noise surrounding China and Australia, the threat of coercion has lurked largely in the background, undebated in detail, at least in public. That has allowed political leaders to avoid focusing on the core issues that will determine whether Beijing decides to discipline a recalcitrant Australia. Namely, how does China itself view economic coercion? What red lines would Australia have to cross to attract sanctions? What are the internal dynamics that prompt China to punish another country? Does Beijing believe such sanctions work, or do they blow back on China, damaging the country's political standing and hurting its economy without achieving the desired end?

On top of that, the three sectors that provide the bulk of Australia's export income from China – resources, education and tourism – all fit into the mainland's economy and society in starkly different ways and are entwined with different constituencies.

China's economic statecraft has been shaped not just by its recent surge in wealth. Beijing has watched for decades how Washington has wielded sanctions against other countries to attempt to bring them to heel. The Chinese remember well how the United States imposed an oil embargo on Imperial Japan in 1941 in response to its occupation of China and South-East Asia. The attack on Pearl Harbor followed soon after. More recently, Washington has routinely used sanctions against other countries and areas, with the current list extending from Russia to the Balkans, Iran, North Korea, Lebanon, Syria and the Democratic Republic of Congo, to name just a few. As a fledgling superpower, Beijing clearly feels it can try the same tactics.

More to the point, Beijing's psyche on this issue was moulded in the decades following the Korean War, when China was subject to a

US embargo itself and forced to rely on trade and technology from the Soviet Union. From the time the Chinese Communist Party took office, its leaders learnt the hard way about how trade could be used as a diplomatic weapon. As Amy King, senior lecturer in strategic and defence studies at the Australian National University, characterises that period: "CCP leaders had not anticipated the US-led embargo, and, when it came, were surprised how quickly it disrupted the Chinese economy."

In the 1950s, King says, Beijing deployed trade as an inducement to drive a wedge between the United States and its allies, such as Japan and the United Kingdom, by offering to open its market to imports.

The use of sanctions is now firmly embedded in mainstream Chinese diplomacy

Beijing's attempt to break the US embargo was also the start of a tradition that has survived into the next century, of an effort to build ties with Asia and Africa and dilute relations with "imperialist" America.

The world looks very different for China today, following its development into an economic behemoth. As a permanent member of the United Nations Security Council, China has joined multilateral sanctions efforts against North Korea and Iran, in both cases primarily under pressure from the United States. Beijing has quietly applied its own sanctions on Pyongyang, both to bring it to the negotiating table and to ensure that its leaders take China's interests into account when they do sit down for talks. In the past, Beijing has both backed and vetoed sanctions against Myanmar at the UN. In tandem with Russia, Beijing has in recent years also blocked UN sanctions against Syria.

Put another way, the use of sanctions is now firmly embedded in mainstream Chinese diplomacy. How, why and when to use them, and on occasion veto them, has been a topic for open debate in Chinese foreign policy circles for more than a decade, and the government has not stepped in to shut it down. In the words of Tsinghua University's Yan Xuetong, well known for his hawkish views, Chinese diplomacy under Xi Jinping is likely to divide the world increasingly along the lines of "friends and enemies". Writing in the early years of the Xi administration, Yan said those countries that play a "constructive" role will get "practical benefits" from China's development. Conversely, antagonistic countries "will face more sanctions and isolation".

Beijing has stuck to the mindset that it pioneered in the early years of the People's Republic, using access to its large market as an inducement to get its way and closing off economic opportunities to countries or companies that don't toe the line. The difference now is that China wields real economic clout as the world's largest trading power. Other countries didn't fear Chinese sanctions in the 1950s. They do now.

But do sanctions work? In the case of South Korea, the target of perhaps the toughest unilateral measures against a close trading partner, there is furious disagreement in Beijing.

Mixed signals on South Korea

It is one thing to stop buying bananas from the Philippines, or salmon from Norway. But when South Korea agreed to a US request to deploy an anti-missile shield in 2016 – the Terminal High Altitude Area Defence (THAAD) system – Beijing was in a bind.

Seoul said the deployment was intended solely to defend it from Pyongyang. Beijing insisted it covered Chinese territory as well, so damaged Chinese security, and demanded it not proceed. In 2017, Seoul stood its ground and installed the system.

South Korea is more than just a neighbour to China. The two countries are indispensable partners in the finely tuned logistical miracle that underpins East Asia's economies. They not only trade together, their interlocking economics and companies make things together as well. In addition, the two countries share mutual security concerns about North Korea and Japan. As a US ally, South Korea is the Asian country most ripe for the picking in China's aim to crack Washington's alliance system in the region. If China is to become the regional hegemon, and push out the United States, it needs South Korea.

Despite these factors, Beijing stuck to its guns, insisting that THAAD was a matter of sovereignty. "This is the dignity that China should have as a major power," said *The People's Daily*, the Chinese Communist Party mouthpiece. Beijing was nonetheless sensitive enough about the issue that it dared not call the sanctions by their name. Rather, as *The People's Daily* explained, it was merely proposed "that Chinese society should voluntarily coordinate in expanding restrictions" on South Korean business.

Such explanations were pure sophistry, as the Chinese state directed a series of damaging actions against its neighbour. Scores of South Korean supermarkets in China were shuttered. Sales of Hyundai cars plummeted, and have never really recovered. Package tours to South Korea were stopped. The shares in Seoul's big entertainment companies dropped sharply. "Let's see how far South Korean TV dramas and stars can go without strong support from the Chinese market," declared *The People's Daily*.

The nation's armchair uber-hawks wanted to go further. China should consider a "surgical" military attack, said Luo Yuan, a regular media commentator, and use "radiation missiles" to destroy THAAD's electronic system. Many mainstream scholars threw their weight behind the measures. "If the United States could enforce sanctions against other countries on issues that have no direct links to its core interests," said Ma Bo of Nanjing University, "China should adopt economic sanctions against South Korea."

The damage wrought by China's ire and its patriotic consumers on South Korean brands and supermarkets attracted most news coverage. But that was far from the whole story. Bilateral trade between the two countries rose during their dispute, largely because China made sure that the most valuable merchandise they bought from South Korea was not touched. Semiconductors and display panels, indispensable inputs into electronic products that have their final assembly in China, were spared. "The cost of exposing workers and factories [in China] relying on imported inputs to manufacture final goods for export was too high," wrote Darren Lim and Victor Ferguson of the Australian National University in an article in East Asia Forum.

Within China itself, the sanctions against an Asian neighbour provoked furious opposition among a sizeable band of scholars. Shen Zhihua, a famous historian of the Cold War and the conflict on the Korean Peninsula, professed himself "disgusted" by the measures. "Don't you have some diplomatic intelligence?" wrote Shen. "You are doing what the enemy wants us to do. You are pushing South Korea to the Japanese and the United States." Deng Yuwen, of the think tank the Charhar Institute, wrote in a similarly despairing vein: "The measures Beijing took only made China–South Korea relations worse. Nothing has changed following THAAD's installation."

> ## Market-driven factors may be more important than geopolitics

How to punish Australia

Australia carries neither the strategic nor the sentimental weight for China that South Korea does. We are not a close neighbour. Nor does China consider Australia to be an Asian country. The mantra that pops up with increasing frequency in China these days – of building an Asia run by Asians – stops at Indonesia. But there are similarities.

Both Australia and South Korea are US allies, and send about one-third of their exports to China, the largest share of any countries in the region. Both also have many goods and services that China, and its citizens, want to buy.

Take iron ore, which is Australia's most valuable commodity largely due to Chinese demand. Chinese steel mills and traders buy about 80 per cent of the iron ore Australia exports. In common parlance, this makes Australia "reliant" on China, a word that immediately positions it as a supplicant, vulnerable to manipulation and bullying. In truth, the two countries are interdependent. Few Australian miners lose sleep in the short term about Beijing cutting iron ore imports to pressure Australia. Along with Brazil, China's other major supplier, Australia has the market locked up, as reliable, high-quality sources are not available elsewhere. "China and Australia are kind of in a multi-scrotum clutch on iron ore," one retired senior Australian mining executive told me. "They are not going to hurt us. We are not going to hurt them." The same goes for metallurgical, or steel-making, coal.

In the longer term, other structural, market-driven factors may be more important than geopolitics. For example, China is investing heavily in steel-arc furnace plants that use scrap metal, rather than iron ore, to make steel. The technology currently accounts for less than 10 per cent of steel production in China, compared to about 50 per cent in the United States. The share of scrap is likely to go up in future, and the use of iron ore, from Australia and elsewhere, will decrease accordingly.

What about liquified natural gas (LNG), over which *The Global Times* sniffed an opportunity to punish Australia? At a glance, LNG is a prime candidate for political interference. In China, the buyers are either state companies, or utilities in a system controlled by the state. The economics of LNG – it is capital intensive, requiring companies to invest billions upfront – means that projects need long-term supply contracts before they go ahead. "China is not the largest market but the fastest-growing large market," a senior Australian LNG executive told me. "So you need China in your portfolio if you have a large project."

All of which in theory gives China leverage – until we hark back to the taunts in *The Global Times* article. There is no small irony in the nationalist tabloid extolling the virtues of importing Russian supplies to place pressure on Australia. The Chinese are as aware as anyone that Russia has long used its position as a dominant gas supplier to coerce other countries on political issues. Moscow has twice interrupted gas supplies to Ukraine, in 2006 and 2009, to put pressure on Kiev. The United States has lobbied Europe to buy less from Russia, precisely because they fear Moscow will use energy as leverage against US allies such as Germany. "Political interference definitely happens. Look how Russia pressured Europe," said the LNG executive. "The Chinese understand that you need to balance Russia." China has already decided as a matter of national policy that it wants more gas and less coal, which in all likelihood means it will not try to cut Australia out of the market.

Thermal coal is a different story. China is largely self-sufficient in coal for its power stations, with imports making up a small proportion of total consumption. But even small Chinese purchases can mean a lot of money for local miners, which is why alarm bells rang in 2019 when Australian cargoes were being turned away from ports in northeast China. DFAT briefed the government and opposition before the election that it believed the cargoes were being blocked on political grounds. Beijing had gotten cleverer on such matters, though, officials said. When they played a similar game with iron ore about a decade ago, they put on paper the instructions for importers and were caught when their diktats leaked. Now such orders are delivered verbally, leaving no paper trail. The Chinese have thus been able to fend off Australian complaints by claiming that the coal is being turned back by port officials on the grounds of quality.

Australian mining officials have a slightly different spin. They agree that Chinese customers are being told not to buy Australian coal. But they say it is about more than just politics. The amount of Australian coal unloaded at Chinese ports is affected by the import quotas set by Beijing's state planners each year, managed by the ports. Commodity traders also had an impact when they attempted to leverage cheaper Australian coal prices against the more expensive local product. As a result, volumes of Australian coal into China have changed little, but the prices, and thus revenues, have dropped substantially. The battle over coal is typical of disputes involving China, with multiple and often overlapping groups in the bureaucracy and business pursuing different agendas and often using politics as a cloak to manipulate markets.

The dynamics of Australia's two other major exports – education and tourism – are very different. China has always tried to micromanage sanctions for maximum impact and minimum blowback. The sort of calibration used for South Korea could also be applied to Australia. Beijing could, for example, slow the rate of tourists or students coming to Australia, while ignoring the bulk of the resources trade, which it needs to power its industrial economy and construction sector.

China has always tried to micromanage sanctions for maximum impact and minimum blowback

As with the wine on the docks in Shanghai, even the slightest disturbance to the number of Chinese studying in Australia can prompt hysterical demands of Canberra. The number of Chinese students starting courses in 2019 increased by only 1.5 per cent, compared to around 7 per cent in 2018, and 17 and 20 per cent in the previous two years.

Such a slowdown might have been welcomed in some quarters. Does it benefit anyone – the universities and their local and foreign students alike – to have Chinese numbers growing by double digits every year? Nonetheless, earlier in 2019 Phil Honeywood of the International Education Association of Australia ploughed headlong into geopolitics in response to the slowing growth in Chinese students, urging multiple federal ministers to find a "circuit breaker" to improve relations. In comments to *The Australian*, Honeywood even weighed in on Canberra's decision to bar Huawei, the Chinese telecommunications company, suggesting it had helped the United Kingdom to recruit students at Australia's expense.

Not all of Honeywood's colleagues in the sector agree that politics has caused the slowdown in Chinese student numbers. "We should not attribute any slowdown in growth out of China to political problems between Canberra and Beijing," one university executive who works with foreign students told me.

Beijing could undoubtedly reduce the numbers of Chinese students moving to Australia. But it would be very hard to stop the flow altogether. The decision to study in Australia is by and large made by an individual and their family, not the government. The United States is already making it tougher for Chinese students to study there. China's relations with Canada are tense due to Huawei, and likely to remain so for some years. The United Kingdom is making a strong push for more Chinese students but has run hot and cold in the past, sharply reducing the number of visas given to foreigners to enter its universities at different times. In such a context, would China want to cut out a major education provider in Australia? The freedom to study overseas represents the fruits of Chinese success, which the government tampers with at its peril.

In addition, most – about 75 per cent – of students are sourced through education agents in China, and Beijing deregulated the system last year. In the past, it would have taken just a few phone calls to agents telling them to restrict students to Australia. Now there are too many agents to call to shut the traffic down so easily. An increasing number of Chinese also enrol to study in Australia on their own, often from outside China itself, bypassing the agent system altogether.

Beijing has had opportunities in the past to stop students from travelling overseas – for example, by restricting the outflow of cash to pay for fees. But it has not done so. Still, "leaving the question hanging can be a useful tactic for China," said Peter Varghese, now chancellor of the University of Queensland, in a 2018 speech. "It makes universities nervous. And that leads some of them to urge the Australian government not to do anything which might annoy China."

There are similarities when it comes to tourism. Again, Beijing has the ability to cut the number of Chinese tourists. It can withdraw a country's status as an approved destination for group tours and informally direct travel agents to avoid certain destinations. It has used such measures to disrupt tourism to the Philippines, and to South Korea, with devastating effect, at a time when nearly half of that country's tourists were from China. In July 2019, Beijing banned individual travel to Taiwan to send a message to the island's leadership. Another weapon is stoking up patriotic anger against an offending country, using the megaphone offered by the state media. As Darren Lim and his co-authors at the Australian National University say in a forthcoming paper: "The most potent tool at the government's disposal is to mobilize, and then direct, the ebbs and flows of Chinese nationalism."

But the tourism market has also been deregulated. Once, almost all Chinese tourists came to Australia on package tours. Increasingly, they travel as individuals and small groups. Once, they would have mostly come from Beijing, Shanghai and Guangzhou, China's most affluent cities. With deregulation, there are now direct flights to Australia from about fifteen Chinese cities, many of which the average Australian might never have heard of, such as Fuzhou and Zhengzhou, catering for the country's burgeoning middle class. Most passengers travel on airlines owned by central and provincial governments, which would suffer substantial losses from the cancellation of routes to Australia. Eleven airlines run direct flights between the two countries, with eight or nine owned by different arms of the Chinese state.

China's red lines

Chris Renwick might be right that Beijing has the whip hand in the China–Australia relationship. During his time as a senior Rio executive, Renwick met Jiang Zemin twice, once when he was Shanghai's mayor, and again when he was head of the Chinese Communist Party. Such meetings are unthinkable these days, because China no longer needs to provide access to its leaders to get the world's attention. The world is trekking to its door anyway.

China's rise, along with Xi Jinping's assertiveness at home and abroad, have changed the geopolitical landscape in countries beyond Australia. Europe – especially Germany and France – Canada and the United States are all struggling with their relationship to China. They are watching how Beijing responds to countries such as Australia, which are pushing back. Smart Australian policy would encourage partnerships that constrain Beijing's ability to punish one democracy without provoking a reaction in another. In a limited sense, this is already in train. The United States, Japan and Australia have long coordinated statements on the South China Sea. The same phenomenon, of democracies speaking with one voice, is spreading to other issues, such as the Uyghurs and Hong Kong.

The biggest constraint on China is the way it is locked into global trade and supply chains. China's globalised economy ensured that Beijing ringfenced its sanctions in the crisis with South Korea. For every country hurt by Chinese import restrictions, there is a party inside China that also suffers economic pain. So far, this equation has helped to stay Beijing's hand in dealing with Australia. "Imposing meaningful costs – in other words, measures which hurt China's economy – has so far been off-limits in almost all cases," Darren Lim told me.

Beijing has the whip hand in the China–Australia relationship

There is little doubt that China has its red lines, which, if crossed, would trigger sanctions. Think Taiwan, or taking sides in a military clash in the South China Sea. Perhaps Beijing is just biding its time with Canberra, but so far Australia doesn't seem to have breached the sanctions threshold.

Still, it would be foolhardy to think that China will not try to extract an economic price at some stage. Beijing is continuing to court Latin American countries, such as Brazil and Argentina, as well as carrying out its Belt and Road Initiative in Eurasia. Both regions are rich in resources and fertile farmlands, qualities that are already proving useful for China as it looks to find new suppliers for products that it now sources from the United States, such as soybeans. China is also building up its own universities in an effort to make foreign institutions less attractive.

Beijing might not be able to tip Canberra into economic depression, but there is little doubt that it has the tools to punish Australia in ways that would hurt employment in the education and tourism sectors, and hit the federal budget, through reducing mineral purchases. Beijing could cause momentary political panic simply by targeting areas of rapidly growing trade, such as meat, wine and vitamins, all industries with the power to lobby Canberra to change policy on China.

Australia may yet pull off the balance of pushing back against China, through greater military spending and anti–foreign interference measures, while increasing bilateral trade. But sooner or later, and well before such an equilibrium is reached, Australia will be tested. It will be at a time and in a sector of Beijing's choosing. Only then will Australians see if talk about getting tough on China is bluster. How much economic pain can Australia and its politics absorb before we wilt? For all the daily noise about China in the media, that is a question this country has only barely started to confront. ◼

HOSTILE TAKEOVER

ASIO's new role as
investment gatekeeper

David Uren

It is hard to credit how swiftly Australia's attitude towards Chinese investment has hardened since the warm embrace of 2014 and early 2015. In quick succession, the Abbott government sealed the free trade agreement, China's President Xi Jinping addressed Australia's parliament, and the government signed up as a founding member of China's regional development initiative, the Asian Infrastructure Investment Bank.

"Truly, no Chinese leader has ever been anything like such a good friend to Australia," the then prime minister, Tony Abbott, said in November 2014, welcoming Xi to Canberra and also drawing attention to his numerous Australian visits to the country. And the strength of the relationship, Abbott said, was sealed not by Australia's role as a primary supplier of the resources building the Chinese nation, but by the flow of investment. "We trade with people when we need them, but we invest with people when we trust them. A relationship might begin with commerce, but it rarely ends there once trust has been established, as I believe it has between Australia and China," he said.

Australia's official investment policy statement on the Foreign Investment Review Board (FIRB) website still opens with "The Australian Government welcomes foreign investment", but the trust proclaimed by Abbott in 2014 has since been heavily qualified. Over the past four years, national security officials – led by the Australian Security and Intelligence Organisation (ASIO) – have played a key role in guiding the management of Australia's official investment relationship with China. And their starting point is one of suspicion.

In its latest annual report, ASIO recorded that it had assessed 245 foreign investment proposals for the FIRB. It said the FIRB had praised "the high quality and continuing improvement of our advice and briefings on the foreign investment threat". Australian officials have not described foreign investment as a "threat" since the economic nationalism of John Gorton's government in the late 1960s.

Behind Australia's darkening perception of Chinese investment is a reappraisal of the nation's administration under Xi Jinping and a new focus on the potential risks flowing from foreign control of economic infrastructure and personal data.

This change is being mirrored globally. A 2019 OECD report stated that since 2017 nine of the world's largest ten economies have adopted new policies to manage security risks involving foreign ownership. It attributed this to a "shift in global economic weights" – a coded reference to the rise of China – as well as heightened sensitivity over control of critical infrastructure and concerns about manipulation of digital technology and diversity of suppliers.

Australia, as the OECD observed, has been a pathbreaker, with innovative legislation that goes beyond simply screening investment as it comes into the country, and is designed to control the risks of foreign involvement in the economy generally.

Open for business

In opposition in 2012, Abbott expressed doubts that state-owned enterprises should ever be allowed to invest, saying, "We don't support the nationalisation of businesses by the Australian government, let alone a foreign one."

The signing of the ChAFTA was followed by a record flow of Chinese investment

But on his first trip to China as prime minister, leading a large business delegation in mid-2014, Abbott declared he hoped for much more Chinese investment on the same basis as other free trade agreement partners. "We now appreciate that most Chinese state-owned enterprises have a highly commercial culture. They're not the nationalised industries that we used to have in Australia."

Throughout 2014, as the Abbott government's energetic trade minister, Andrew Robb, worked to seal a trade deal with China, the focus was on how to liberalise the rules governing foreign investment.

Australia's main interest was greater access to Chinese markets for agriculture and services. China wanted more flexibility for its firms to invest in Australia without running the gauntlet of the FIRB.

Abbott was considering China's request that the A$1 billion threshold for screening investments from free trade partners apply to both private and state-owned Chinese enterprises. State-owned firms would not need FIRB approval if they could establish they were essentially "commercial" in their operations. This would have been a radical move. In the aftermath of the financial crisis, even investments in Australia by US banks and motor-vehicle companies required government approval, because the US government had taken an equity interest in them.

It proved too hard to craft provisions for state enterprises in the China–Australia Free Trade Agreement (ChAFTA) ahead of Xi's November 2014 visit, and the issue was shelved for review.

Treasurer Joe Hockey said the Chinese were interested in practical outcomes, and the reality was that the FIRB was now treating Chinese state-owned companies on a commercial basis. "I've consulted with our security agencies about the risks and formed the view that some SOEs [state-owned enterprises] in general were no greater risk to Australia's national interest than investment from private companies, some of which are more closely wedded to the interests of a foreign state than a state-owned company might be," he said in late 2014. He said the FIRB's approval of an A$6 billion purchase by the State Grid Corporation of China – 20 per cent of energy company

SP AusNet and 60 per cent of its related Jemena electricity networks – reflected the Abbott government's more liberal approach to Chinese government-owned business.

The signing of the ChAFTA and the open warmth in relations between the Abbott and Xi governments was followed by a record flow of Chinese investment. The FIRB approved proposed investments totalling $47 billion in 2016 – a 70 per cent increase on 2014 levels. Monitoring of transactions by the Australian National University's East Asian Bureau of Economic Research showed the value of deals concluded in 2016 almost tripling, to $16 billion.

This influx generated friction. Up to 30,000 Chinese housing investments were being recorded annually by the FIRB. Although by law foreign residents could only purchase newly built properties, this restriction was thought to be widely flouted, as the FIRB lacked staff to enforce it. In the popular media, it was suggested that Chinese buyers were driving up house prices, putting them out of reach of first-home buyers. The National Party was also hostile to Chinese investment in farmland and had committed to tightening controls.

Goaded by these pressures, the Abbott government embarked on the first comprehensive rewrite of the *Foreign Acquisitions and Takeovers Act* since it was legislated by the Fraser government in 1975. The revised act imposed fees on foreign investment applications, designed to fund much tougher enforcement, which was to be conducted by the Australian Tax Office. The threshold for FIRB approval of agricultural land and related food industries was sharply reduced, while the overall approach was much more prescriptive, with less scope for discretion by the Treasury officers who handled foreign investment applications.

The consultation for these amendments led both the ATO and national security officials to give deeper consideration to the foreign investment approval process. They approached it with suspicion – the ATO believing that investors were out to evade tax, and security officials believing national interests were threatened.

Darwin anxieties

The lease of Darwin's port to the private Chinese group Landbridge in October 2015 marked a watershed in Australia's approach to foreign investment. The Northern Territory government had been fretting about the port since 2013, as traffic was increasing and it appeared likely to hit full capacity. The Territory lacked the resources to upgrade it and the federal government had declined to finance it, so the government set about finding a private operator.

The transaction did not require FIRB approval, as it was the lease rather than the purchase of a government asset. Yet the Northern Territory government consulted the board and the defence and intelligence services before the deal was finalised. The federal cabinet's national security committee was also aware of the transaction.

Defence officials were emphatic that they held no concerns. The then department secretary, Dennis Richardson, said the lease had been considered by the Australian Signals Directorate, the Defence security agency and the department's strategic policy unit. "No part of defence had a concern from a security perspective in respect of the sale," he said. The head of the defence forces, Air Chief Marshal Mark Binskin, told a Senate inquiry that the leasehold would make no difference to China's ability to monitor shipping. "I can sit at the fish and chip shop on the wharf at the moment in Darwin and watch ships come and go, regardless of who owns it [the port]."

Not everyone was so relaxed. The executive director of the Australian Strategic Policy Institute (ASPI), Peter Jennings, wrote in *The Australian* that "Australia's strategic interests, including responding to increasingly assertive Chinese maritime behaviour in the South and East China seas, now have to be balanced against

Security officials were worried that [Turnbull] would not take China's apparent threat to national security seriously

the reality of operating out of a harbour run by a company whose website proclaims it is 'contributing its best to ... realising the great rejuvenation of the Chinese dream'".

There is no doubt that Jennings' concerns about the Darwin lease were shared by some in the defence and intelligence communities, despite the official response. Jennings felt defence was looking at the narrow issue of whether it would have continuing access to the port, not at the long-term implications. He argued that the port would be used by the Royal Australian Navy to defend Australia's northern approaches and that Australian forces could be required to mount operations to counter China out of a port run by a Chinese company.

Jennings' concerns were shared by the US government, which had committed to base up to 2500 marines in Darwin. *The Australian Financial Review* reported that US president Barack Obama told then prime minister Malcolm Turnbull that the United States should have been given a "heads up" about the deal. Andrew Krepinevich, a prominent US military strategist and member of the chief of naval operations' advisory board, said the deal was short-sighted. At worst, "it threatens to undermine Australia's relations with its closest security partner, the US, at a time when the latter is finally beginning to put serious effort behind its pivot to the Asia-Pacific".

The US embassy conducted what appeared to be a "push poll" of Australian opinion, leaking the results, which it said showed the Darwin port lease would "likely force Australians to rethink their choices of when to put national security ahead of economic gain".

Turnbull changes tune

When Malcolm Turnbull overthrew Tony Abbott to claim the prime ministership in August 2015, security officials were reportedly worried that he would not take China's apparent threat to national security seriously. It was "probably the first time since Whitlam where we have had a prime minister where we don't know where he stands on national security grounds", an unnamed official was quoted as saying in *The Australian Financial Review*.

But new currents soon started to reshape Australia's relationship with China.

Abbott had seen Xi as a modernising leader who was getting tough on corruption and promising reform, and who might even lead the nation to a form of democracy. By 2016, the Turnbull government viewed the Chinese administration in a much harsher light.

It is hard to identify a single catalyst for the change. China's military installations in the South China Sea were a source of friction with the United States and its allies, Australia's embassy in Beijing was doubtless reporting tighter censorship and the mass detention of Uighur people in China's west, and there was alarm over cyber intrusions, including a major disruption of the Bureau of Meteorology that Australian authorities reportedly attributed to "state actors".

The Darwin deal was completed two months after Turnbull became prime minister. In response to the concerns about the lease, the foreign investment regulations were amended to ensure that future transactions involving "critical infrastructure", whether this infrastructure was government-owned or not, would be referred to the FIRB.

In late 2015, Turnbull's new treasurer, Scott Morrison, announced the appointment of David Irvine to the board of the FIRB. Irvine's impressive CV included heading each of the major intelligence agencies, ASIO and ASIS (the Australian Secret Intelligence Service), and serving as Australia's ambassador to China in the early 2000s. "In the years ahead, it will be increasingly important for FIRB to not only have the commercial expertise and background to deal with complex commercial transactions, but to also have an even greater understanding of the broader strategic issues, including national security issues, that are essential to protect our national interest," Morrison said.

In a further indication of the Turnbull government's hardening approach, Morrison announced decisions to block two Chinese investments. The first was the Kidman cattle properties in South Australia, West Australia, Queensland and the Northern Territory, which covered 100,000 square kilometres. Although a financial minnow, with annual sales of less than $70 million, it was the largest private landholding in the country. One of the Kidman properties overlapped with the Woomera Prohibited Area in South Australia, and Morrison indicated that this was a problem with a Chinese buyer. The property was in the lowest-security "green zone", some 650 kilometres away from the Woomera base. Morrison said he would reconsider the deal if that property were removed. When the vendors restructured the sale to exclude this property, Morrison still had concerns about the size of the holdings, covering 1.3 per cent of Australia's landmass, leading the Chinese buyer to withdraw.

The then chair of the FIRB, investment banker David Wilson, told an Australia China Business Council forum that the sale had captured public attention because it was "so iconic and so large". "I'd suggest that if you are a [Chinese company] looking to invest, that you try to avoid icons," he said.

The second vetoed deal was more substantial. The privatisation of New South Wales' power distribution business, Ausgrid, had been in the works for over a year, and the government had strong bids of more than A$10 billion from the Chinese state-owned company State Grid Corporation and the private Hong Kong firm CKI. A few days before the final tender deadline, Morrison announced that foreign bids could not be accepted. He said that during the review, national security issues were identified in "critical power and communications services" and that there was no possible mitigation of the risks. Asked at a press conference to elaborate, he replied, "The only person in the room with security clearance to hear that answer is me."

Xi was on a mission to "engineer the souls" of the Chinese people

Advisers to the deal had been expecting approval and were shocked, as was the New South Wales government. It had long been known that Ausgrid supplied power to the Lucas Heights nuclear reactor, to the Garden Island naval base and to the microwave dishes on the Sydney Tower. *The Sydney Morning Herald*'s Peter Hartcher reported that the Australian Signals Directorate, the government's electronic intelligence agency, had realised that Ausgrid hosted infrastructure crucial to the joint United States and Australian Pine Gap communications station outside Alice Springs. People close to the transaction maintain it is implausible that this was not known from the outset and suggest there must have been a deeper, darker secret, possibly involving Australian espionage of which even allies were unaware, that came to light at the last minute.

Whatever the cause, the collapse of the deal was an embarrassment to all concerned. It prompted the government to establish a "critical infrastructure centre", which would compile and manage a database of all sensitive infrastructure to ensure such a mistake could not happen again. The centre would provide risk assessments to assist foreign investment decisions. It would also address growing concerns in Canberra that internet-based industrial control systems were susceptible to cyberattack – Russia had shut down Ukraine's electricity system in December 2015, while the United States had used a cyberattack to disable much of Iran's nuclear enrichment capacity in 2010.

The centre, which was launched in January 2017, was followed by new legislation that empowers it to demand a wide range of confidential commercial information. This includes details about the ownership and corporate governance of infrastructure, and operational information including outsourcing arrangements. The legislation gives the government broad powers to direct operational decisions. Separate legislation was also developed for the telecommunications industry.

The OECD says Australia's laws break new ground in managing security risks in the operation, as distinct from acquisition, of a business. "The availability of means to intervene ... may give governments comfort to allow acquisitions that they would otherwise have prohibited for fear that the ownership could become problematic later," it stated.

The circumstances of the Kidman and the Ausgrid investment vetoes were too idiosyncratic to imply any comprehensive change of stance towards Chinese investment, but attitudes were toughening both within the government and the security agencies.

ASIO steps in

Malcolm Turnbull had hired *The Sydney Morning Herald*'s former China correspondent, John Garnaut, as a media adviser before shifting him to provide advice on foreign affairs. Garnaut, the son of Bob Hawke's economic adviser and former Chinese ambassador Ross Garnaut, had developed a deeply pessimistic view of the Xi Jinping administration.

Garnaut suggested that Xi was on a mission, lifted from Josef Stalin, to "engineer the souls" of the Chinese people in an exercise of absolutist totalitarianism. "Xi's project of total ideological control does not stop at China's borders. It is packaged to travel with Chinese students, tourists, migrants and especially money," he argued in a 2017 speech to officials from the Department of Prime Minister and Cabinet.

In August 2016, Turnbull commissioned Garnaut to lead an ASIO review of China's intelligence and "interference" activities in Australia. It paved the way for sweeping new espionage and foreign interference legislation. A new offence of "theft of trade secrets on behalf of a foreign government" was introduced, along with new rules to govern relationships between Australian officials and anyone representing a foreign interest. It included a demand that lobbyists register as "foreign agents".

Turnbull left the Chinese in no doubt that the legislation was directed at them by paraphrasing the statement Mao Zedong was believed to have used to found the Chinese republic. "The Australian people stand up," he told the media in Mandarin.

Although the legislation was primarily about stopping improper influence on Australian democratic processes, to avoid a situation such as the Russian manipulation of the 2016 US presidential election, ASIO made it clear that the laws were also designed to cover improper activities by foreign investors. ASIO's annual reports had never mentioned foreign investment before the 2014–15 edition, but have become discursive on the topic since. The latest says the threat of foreign investment extends beyond critical infrastructure, noting that ASIO has been raising government awareness of wider concerns such as data protection and foreign powers' use of investment for espionage, foreign interference or sabotage.

"The threat is no longer only about access to critical infrastructure and associated data," it states. "For example, foreign intelligence services could use the ownership and the access provided through foreign investment to influence key decision-makers in the Australian government and/or manipulate suppliers and customers during business decisions."

This is an expansive view of the risks involved in foreign investment. Foreign companies, including state-owned businesses, have
always lobbied governments about matters of regulation and taxa-
tion influencing their business, without thinking they were in any way
impinging upon national security.

In April 2017, a little over a year after appointing David Irvine
to the board of the FIRB, Morrison made him the chair. It was
the first time the FIRB had been led by someone with a national
security background. The board
had traditionally been chaired by
a banker or a businessman – its
focus had been mainly on competition and industry structure.

Authorities are now pushing for all directors in data-sensitive businesses to be Australian

The seven-member board
still has deep business experience, including lawyer and
company director Cheryl Edwardes, former Rio Tinto Australia
managing director David Peever, and Seven West Media director and
former Deloitte partner Teresa Dyson. However, lawyers specialised
in foreign investment matters say that since Irvine's appointment,
the board has become more attentive to the concerns of the security
agencies.

Following advice from ASIO, the government said in February
2018 that it would consider the need for "ownership diversity"
when reviewing foreign investments in the electricity industry.

Nine months later, treasurer Josh Frydenberg cited a lack of owner-ship diversity as a reason for blocking an A$13 billion bid for the energy business APA Group by Hong Kong's CKI. APA is Australia's biggest gas pipeline business, controlling 56 per cent of Australia's pipelines. Frydenberg said the FIRB had been unable to come to a unanimous recommendation and he had sought the advice of the Critical Infrastructure Centre. This implies that some members of the board had accepted the Australian Competition and Consumer Commission's finding that the takeover would not endanger compe-tition, subject to undertakings that CKI had given to divest assets. However Frydenberg said the ACCC had not considered the con-centration of foreign ownership and it appears he listened to the national security advice.

The impact of national security concerns has been most keenly felt in relation to investments involving personal data, such as in the health, retail and financial services sectors. ASIO does not accept that ownership structures such as limited partnerships mitigate the risks. It assumes that ownership of a business enables access to its data. The FIRB, on national security advice, is imposing strict conditions where data is involved in an acquisition, including that a majority of directors must be Australian resident citizens, with some clearly independent. At least one must have a security clearance. The idea is that there should be someone on the board with whom the gov-ernment can have a confidential discussion. The FIRB then requires that director to chair a security committee, which will typically include the CFO and the firm's security manager. The committee must report both to the government and to the board. Compliance must be audited, with the auditor replaced ever three years.

Investment advisers say the new security concerns are building long delays into the approvals. In one case, a proposed independent director died before his security clearance came through.

Security authorities are now pushing for all directors in data-sensitive businesses to be Australian citizens. This would, if successful, eliminate much of the point of foreign investment, which is to introduce foreign expertise, as well as money, to a business.

The Huawei ban

The Turnbull government's concerns about Chinese participation in the economy reached a crescendo on its last day in office, with the decision to ban Chinese telecommunications firms Huawei and ZTE from participation in the rollout of the 5G internet network. Australia was the first major country to implement such a ban, with the United States following in May 2019. The United Kingdom and Germany have both decided the risks of Huawei's participation can be managed, while Canada was waiting until after its October election to announce its stance.

The Gillard government had previously banned Huawei from participating in the NBN rollout on the advice of the security agencies, amid fears it could insert secret "back doors" into the network that would compromise data security. But the firm believed it had a strong claim to participate in the 5G network with its globally leading technology.

With 4G, Huawei was excluded from providing technology for the core network but was allowed to provide peripheral equipment. The question is whether such a separation is possible for the 5G network (the United Kingdom and Germany believe it is). Both the Department of Foreign Affairs under Julie Bishop and the Department of Communications under Mitch Fifield were pushing for the Chinese operators to be allowed to participate in peripheral technology, subject to conditions, potentially similar to those applied in the United Kingdom, where Huawei funds independent inspection of its technology. Turnbull had been sympathetic and asked the Australian Signals Directorate to develop an option to allow it.

Home affairs minister Peter Dutton was strongly opposed. At a cabinet meeting held amid high leadership tension, Dutton's hard line prevailed. The then ASD director-general, Mike Burgess, decided that his department's work on a safeguard system was insufficient and sided with his counterpart at ASIO, Duncan Lewis, in supporting an outright ban. With the key security agencies opposed, the rest of cabinet fell into line.

Burgess (who was appointed to replace Lewis as ASIO director-general in August 2019) told the Australian Strategic Policy Institute at the time that in the past Australia had confined "high-risk vendors" to supplying peripheral equipment. "But the distinction between core and edge collapses in 5G networks. That means that a potential threat anywhere in the network will be a threat to the whole network."

The formulation used to exclude Huawei reflected the influence of US intelligence authorities, who pointed to a Chinese law that requires organisations to assist state security agencies in pursuit of counterespionage work.

It fell to Morrison to announce the ban, as acting home affairs minister (Dutton had resigned from cabinet following his initial unsuccessful challenge for the prime ministership). Morrison was flanked by Fifield, who resigned immediately afterwards. There was concern that it would be a bad look for such a decision to be announced by two acting ministers.

National security bodies only see foreign investment as a threat to be managed

Morrison did not mention Huawei or ZTE by name but said there was a history of cyberattacks on Australia and the government had found no satisfactory way to mitigate the risks. He stated involving vendors who are likely subject to directions from a foreign government that conflict with Australian law may risk unauthorised access or interference.

This explanation avoided repeating unsubstantiated claims about Huawei manipulating technology to suit the Chinese state or flaring a debate about private and state-owned companies. The fact that China could demand Huawei meet the requests of its security agencies was enough.

Australia and the United States will obtain their 5G networks from the Scandinavian companies Ericsson and Nokia. It is not yet clear to what extent Huawei's ambitions for global 5G leadership will be damaged by US technology export bans.

Security versus treasury

Despite the intense security focus, Chinese firms are continuing to invest in Australia. They are building solar and wind farms, buying health centres and adding to their agricultural assets. The Reserve Bank notes that in addition to direct investment, Chinese banks in Australia have extended credit to businesses totalling A$35 billion. Although only a small share of total business lending, it is more than the loan books of US banks in Australia and is comparable with the lending of Japanese and European banks.

The flow of investment has plunged from its 2016 peak. This is partly due to tightened Chinese capital controls, though it is always hard to attribute definitive reasons for lost investment. The value of FIRB applications halved to A$24 billion in 2018, while the East Asian Bureau of Economic Research database at the Australian National University shows the deals concluded last year totalled less than a third of the peak, at just A$5 billion. Chinese investment worldwide was down 18 per cent in 2018.

It was announced in early 2017 that the China–Australia Foreign Trade Agreement was so successful that the review scheduled for 2018 had been brought forward by twelve months. This review was supposed to revisit the investment chapter. But, within months, official relations between the two countries were frozen and the renegotiation was stillborn.

In the lead-up to the 2019 federal election, former prime minister Paul Keating blamed the security agencies for the deterioration in Australia's relationship with China. "When the security agencies are running foreign policy, the nutters are in charge. They've lost their strategic bearings, these organisations," he said.

The intelligence agencies were taking their lead, he believed, from Turnbull's adviser. "Once that Garnaut guy came back from China and Turnbull gave him the ticket to go and hop into the security agencies, they've all gone berko ever since."

Politicians from both sides either condemned or distanced themselves from these remarks. Morrison called on Labor leader Bill Shorten to denounce the "Labor legend" and Shorten said he respectfully disagreed with Keating. Keating was the first to draw public attention – with his characteristic colour – to the ascendance of the national security agencies over the Department of Foreign Affairs and Trade in shaping Australia's relationship with its major economic partner. The bypassing of DFAT has become more acute with the concentration of intelligence agencies in the new super-department of Home Affairs under Peter Dutton.

A recent paper from the University of Sydney's United States Studies Centre argues that national security should be the only grounds for vetting foreign investment, and that Treasury should play no role. Authors Stephen Kirchner and Jared Mondschein argue that concerns about competition, tax or environmental impacts would be dealt with competently by domestic agencies.

They suggest that security should only constrain foreign investment in limited circumstances, including where it could affect supplies critical to defence or the broader economy, or could lead to risky technology or data transfer to foreign interests or to threats of infiltration, surveillance or sabotage. But they argue there are few markets where attempts to restrict supply could cause lasting damage, while risks over technology and data can mostly be mitigated without rejecting acquisitions. Threats of more classic espionage are better controlled with security screening of staff and managers than owners. They call for the FIRB to develop a set of clear principles for guiding businesses on security concerns and say it should report directly to cabinet's national security committee, not the treasurer.

ASPI's Jennings has similarly argued that final decision-making on foreign investment should rest with the national security committee. He says the current arrangement "puts the treasurer into a difficult position of, from time to time, having to make decisions on national security matters without the Treasury currently having the expertise to advise on these areas".

But it is unlikely that the national security agencies would ever agree to be bound by a narrow set of principles, as Kirchner and Mondschein suggest. The intelligence community believes the threats it confronts are constantly mutating and the national security agencies require the flexibility to define them and the responses as they see fit.

The problem is that national security bodies only see foreign investment as a threat to be managed. They have neither the interest nor the capacity to assess the positive influence of foreign investment on business development, employment or economic growth. The experience of the past five years shows their definition of that threat is ever expanding – the potential for foreign executives to lobby government officials is the latest grounds for concern. In an interconnected world, the web of worrisome connections is never-ending from a security perspective.

Security concerns about Chinese investment are only likely to become stronger

Amid sharpening geopolitical tensions between the United States and China, Australia's national security concerns about Chinese investment are only likely to become stronger. It is important that the national security voice remains contested. The FIRB should retain strong business representation to make the positive case for foreign investment. Anyone who has sat on a company board understands the difference between ownership and control. They have daily experience of the robustness of our political system against lobbyists. And they understand the importance of keeping Australia open to global investment.

Treasury's continued control of final decision-making over foreign investment is essential. It is only from the economic perspective carried by Treasury that foreign investment is truly welcomed for its contribution to the wealth and prosperity of the nation, now and into the future. ■

BOUGAINVILLE'S QUEST FOR INDEPENDENCE

A special report
on the referendum

Ben Bohane

In May 1994, the island of Bougainville was in the midst of a brutal ten-year conflict. I found myself with the rebel leader, Francis Ona, head of the Bougainville Revolutionary Army (BRA), in his village above the destroyed Panguna mine site. Below us spread an industrial apocalypse – one of the world's most advanced copper and gold mines torched beyond repair, as men scavenged materials to create home-made weapons in armouries set up next to huge, rusting mining trucks.

Ona said to me solemnly, in words I would never forget: "We are at war with Australia ... but it is not our intention. We wish Australia could be neutral, but instead they continue to support the Papua New Guinea Defence Force."

I'd run the naval blockade imposed by the Papua New Guinea Defence Force (PNGDF) to report for *Time* magazine on a guerrilla war on Australia's doorstep that had received very little attention.

The war had started when the first cell of BRAs, led by Ona, a former surveyor, attacked the Panguna mine with explosives and forced the closure of what was considered the most advanced copper and gold mine in the world. Bougainvilleans had a long list of grievances, including the tiny royalties they received from the mine, the pollution it caused, and social problems brought by Papua New Guinean mainlanders who came to work here. Ona claimed there was growing fear that the whole island would be dug up for mining and Bougainvilleans would be forced to resettle elsewhere.

After spending a month with BRA guerrillas I returned the following year, for balance, to accompany the PNGDF as they and their local militia, the Bougainville Resistance Force (BRF), tried to wrest back control of the island. Several more trips were to follow, covering the war but also the peace – as Australia and New Zealand cobbled together a series of regional peacekeeping initiatives that would provide a template for later Pacific interventions in Timor-Leste and Solomon Islands.

Ultimately, Bougainville's war, which stretched from 1988 to 1998, is thought to have claimed at least 10,000 lives. It also destroyed the infrastructure of Papua New Guinea's most prosperous province.

The sentiment Ona expressed in his village – that Australia unfairly sided with Port Moresby during the war – remains strong on

Bougainville. It could be a stumbling block as Canberra tries to develop a new, more neutral policy while this island group heads towards independence.

Twenty-one years since the end of the war – the most serious conflict in the South Pacific since World War II – this island group of 300,000 people to the far east of Papua New Guinea is preparing for a referendum on independence that will likely see a clear majority vote yes to *bruklus* ("break away") from Papua New Guinea. Historically and culturally, Bougainvilleans claim their traditional links were mostly with people of the western Solomon Islands rather than the Papua New Guinean mainland: they looked "east" rather than "west". Another

Whether the Marape government is open to recognising a yes vote remains to be seen

important feature of Bougainville society is that it is matrilineal – women own the land, not men. In many ways it was women who helped trigger the war and women who helped end it. They now play an important role in shaping Bougainville's future.

When I returned in January 2019 to gauge sentiment on the island, it was difficult to find anyone who wanted it to remain part of Papua New Guinea. A combination of strong Bougainvillean ethno-identity, anger from the war years and consideration of Papua New Guinea's current (particularly economic) dilemmas have all pushed Bougainvilleans towards this moment – their opportunity to, on

23 November 2019, vote for independence.

If the vote passes, this territory – which was administered by Australia for sixty years, between 1915 and Papua New Guinea's independence in 1975 – might become the next new nation in the world and the first in our region since the liberation of Timor-Leste.

Although the November referendum is a high point, it is not the end point. Nor is the outcome guaranteed. According to the roadmap set out by the Bougainville Peace Agreement signed by all major factions in 2001, the result must be ratified by the Papua New Guinea parliament (effectively giving Papua New Guinea a veto), and the final status of Bougainville will be negotiated between the Papua New Guinea government and the Autonomous Bougainville Government. Will Papua New Guinea honour the result or seek to delay proceedings? If delayed, how long before hardliners in Bougainville make another unilateral declaration of independence, as they did in 1975 and again in 1991? Such a situation may prompt another regional security crisis, especially if some countries – including China – recognise such a declaration to try to gain a foothold in the South Pacific.

The new Marape government in Port Moresby has shown signs that it is more willing to engage with the peace process, releasing funds for a referendum and appointing Sir Puka Temu as the minister for Bougainville affairs, a decision that went down well in the island group. Bougainville president John Momis had spent several exasperating years trying to get now former PNG prime minister

"Francis Ona said to me solemnly, in words I would never forget: 'We are at war with Australia.'"

Peter O'Neill to deliver promised funding for the referendum, even accusing the government of trying to "sabotage" the peace process. Whether the Marape government is open to recognising a yes vote remains to be seen, but it has at least taken a more balanced approach so far.

Australia must try to keep the peace process on track, without being seen to favour either side. During the war, Australia was not neutral – it supplied the PNGDF with helicopters, which were quickly turned into gunships, and continued to train and equip soldiers. Its reputation remains tarnished by the impacts of mining and colonialism, but there is still goodwill due to its role in the peacekeeping operations.

"The future of the dormant Panguna mine
has already caused deep divisions."

Australia will potentially recognise the outcome of the vote, though among Bougainvilleans there remains lingering suspicion: Australia has made no public statements to signal it is "neutral" towards Bougainville sovereignty, so many assume it is still pro–Papua New Guinea.

This is creating confusion about Australia's relationship with a future independent Bougainville. It comes as China has made its own position clear, promising US$1 billion for investments and to assist Bougainville with its "transition". In December last year a delegation of ten Chinese visitors met with various local leaders, offering assistance and investment in mining, tourism and agriculture. A new port in Bana district was mooted, even though Bougainville already has two functioning ports along its east coast. It is uncertain how "official" the Chinese delegation was, or how much of the proposed offer involves grants as opposed to loans, but the signal was clear – China is ready to "assist".

There are other players in the geopolitical mix. Indonesia is worried that an independent Bougainville could set a regional precedent for West Papua, where many local Papuans are also pushing for a referendum on independence.

For Australia and Papua New Guinea, the policy options are more limited than two decades ago. A clear vote for independence will be difficult to ignore. Where once Australia was the key power in the region, **Australia has an opportunity to help resolve the status of this disputed territory** today Pacific nations have more agency. China's growing ties are giving the islands added leverage. Other Pacific nations such as Solomon Islands, Fiji and Vanuatu, which have been involved in peacekeeping operations on Bougainville, are watching closely to determine their response. This is no longer a domestic issue for Papua New Guinea, but a regional and an international one. The United Nations, which has maintained an office in Bougainville for more than twenty years, is also involved in maintaining the peace and overseeing the referendum, and has an envoy reporting directly to the UN secretary-general.

So far, the referendum process has been largely peaceable, but it faces risks. Bougainvilleans will keep the peace so long as they can see the roadmap being implemented. They feel they have paid a "blood sacrifice" over the past century and are ready to rule themselves. As they are sitting on large reserves of copper and gold, rich fishing grounds and land with a history of agricultural production (especially cocoa), Bougainville has the resources and skills to become a viable independent nation. Yet this depends on local leaders maintaining a sense of broad unity, and building political integrity and consensus around mining issues. They will also need to educate a "lost generation", which grew up during the war.

There are myriad challenges – the future of the dormant Panguna mine, in particular, has already caused deep divisions. No one is sure what the transition period will look like if a yes vote is ratified by Papua New Guinea. As a possible model, some have referred to the UN mission in Timor-Leste, where a transitional administration governed for three years before full sovereignty was achieved.

Ideally Bougainville's political status should be resolved within the Pacific family. Australia, along with New Zealand, should act as "honest brokers" and help to nudge all sides towards a final settlement, rather than allow long-running resentments to fester, which could result in more distant powers such as China increasing their involvement. Australia and New Zealand can be proud of their role in deploying unarmed peacekeepers (almost unheard of in the annals of international peacekeeping) and allowing *kastom* reconciliation

"[Bougainvilleans] feel they have paid a 'blood sacrifice' over the past century and are ready to rule themselves."

processes to occur, including local ceremonies where former militants line up to break bows and arrows, shake hands and chew betel nut together. These events put local communities and culture at the heart of the peace process and have become something of a model for conflict resolution elsewhere.

In the lead-up to the referendum, Australia needs to play an even hand but also to signal to the Bougainville people that it is now genuinely neutral towards Bougainville's possible statehood. It will be difficult for Australia, Papua New Guinea and the rest of the region to deny the island group's aspirations without creating a fresh crisis.

There remains unfinished business here. Australia has an opportunity to help resolve the status of this disputed territory within the

Pacific family and to move past its previous complicity in the war. Francis Ona died in 2005 but his ghost still hovers over the island, a potent figure of nationalism and resistance. Bougainville's leaders want to be at peace with Australia – and Papua New Guinea – without the need to resist again. ■

THE FIX

Solving Australia's foreign affairs challenges

—

Melissa Conley Tyler on How to Rebuild Australia's Diplomatic Capacity

"The Department of Foreign Affairs and Trade has been systematically underfunded for at least a decade. Its budget must be increased to enable it to promote Australia's interests in the world."

THE PROBLEM: Australia has run down its diplomatic capacity to the point that it is under-resourced to confront current foreign policy challenges.

Despite the talents and dedication of its staff, we risk a situation where the primary duties of the Department of Foreign Affairs and Trade will be issuing passports, providing consular assistance and managing ministerial visits. This would limit Australia's ability to prosecute its interests abroad, leaving it hostage to international forces rather than trying to shape them.

Where once Australia had a relatively benign foreign policy environment, it now faces an increasingly complex one.

The challenges are set out eloquently in the 2017 Foreign Policy White Paper, including great power competition, climate change and rapid technological change. This is an era in which the stability of the Indo-Pacific region cannot be assumed and the rules and institutions that help maintain peace and security are under strain.

And yet while the White Paper calls for bold action, no new funds were allocated to DFAT to achieve this. The national president of the Australian Institute of International Affairs, Allan Gyngell, described it as "magical thinking, no resources". Despite warnings over the past decade of DFAT's chronic under-funding, including in the Lowy Institute reports *Diplomatic Deficit* (2009) and *Diplomatic Disrepair* (2011), there has been a bipartisan neglect of Australia's diplomacy, and repeated cuts to the DFAT budget.

Australia's combined budget for diplomacy and aid has contracted from A$8.3 billion for the 2013–14 financial year (adjusted for inflation) to A$6.7 billion for 2019–20. The foreign aid budget is A$4 billion, down A$1 billion since 2013, and at its lowest point ever as a percentage of gross national income at 0.2 per cent.

In 2017, Australia was ranked twentieth of twenty-nine among developed nations in the OECD (Organisation for Economic Co-operation and Development) for its diplomatic resources. With 116 diplomatic missions abroad, Australia is below the OECD average of 132, and nowhere near the G20 average of 194. It is beaten by countries such as Portugal, Greece and Chile, which have smaller populations and less than 20 per cent of Australia's GDP.

And even these figures overstate Australia's reach: many of its diplomatic posts are micro-missions, with as few as two or three staff posted from Canberra, meaning they have limited outreach and spend much of their time on administration. The ever-growing number of Australians travelling abroad has meant an increase in the proportion of funding allocated for passport applications and consular assistance (now 23 per cent of DFAT's budget) at the cost of its broader diplomatic mission. Given the complexity and scale of issues it faces in the fast-moving international environment, DFAT's funding is beyond lean. This has implications for recruitment and retention of talented staff.

THE PROPOSAL: The federal government must commit to increasing the resources available to DFAT, immediately raising the department's budget to at least 1.5 per cent of the federal budget. There are two relevant comparisons that would justify this increase.

First, we can compare current spending with that during a period when Australia faced a similar international outlook: after World War II, when a new global order was being built.

As Asialink professorial fellow Tony Milner puts it, Australia today is even more lonely than it was then, with the influence of the West in the region in decline and power dynamics shifting. In 1949, the combined diplomacy, trade and aid budget was almost 9 per cent of the federal budget, reducing to 3.2 per cent by 1969, 1.9 per cent by 1989, 1.5 per cent by 2009, then to the current 1.3 per cent.

Second, Australia can compare itself to other developed countries with similar-sized economies. Canada, for instance, spends 1.92 per cent of its national budget on diplomacy and aid; the Netherlands spends 4.33 per cent. Australia should invest more than these countries, which arguably have an easier task. As former Australian ambassador John McCarthy has noted, Australia needs to forge relationships with neighbours with diverse histories and cultures. This makes it a difficult diplomatic patch.

These comparisons suggest a budget target of at least 1.5 per cent as an immediate measure, with a view to raising it further. This would be an increase of A$900 million, from A$6.7 billion to A$7.6 billion. Without this, it is unlikely that DFAT will be able to successfully navigate the foreign policy challenges outlined in the 2017 White Paper.

If nothing else, DFAT should be granted an exemption from the efficiency dividend until its budget rises to a more normal historical level. This measure, usually levied at 1 to 1.25 per cent of the administrative budget, reached 4 per cent in 2012–13. With DFAT cut to the bone, the focus should be on increasing its budget, not constant cuts.

WHY IT WILL WORK: Extra investment in diplomacy will expand Australia's ability to promote its security and prosperity in concrete, measurable ways.

Increased funding would allow the Australia Awards scholarships scheme to be expanded, ensuring that other nations' leaders have studied and built ties in Australia. This program has already been a huge source of influence and soft power. For example, a quarter of Mongolia's cabinet are Australia Awards alumni. These scholarships mean that regional leaders are more positively disposed towards Australia, rather than having formed links with other countries. Australia currently grants thirty scholarships to Laos each year, while China grants around 1000.

Increased funding would also enable diplomats to reach influential people in target nations better to shape their views on Australia, whether through meetings, events or public diplomacy. This helps to develop personal and organisational linkages and to send messages about Australia to relevant audiences. It would allow diplomatic missions to identify and sponsor more people to come to Australia on special and international media visits.

Increased funding would boost business promotion, with tangible results for Australia's economy and jobs. This includes building closer relationships with potential investors and with consumers through campaigns such as Taste of Australia, which showcases Australian producers. If Australia doesn't have a diplomat based in a country – or if there's such a small mission that there's no time for anything except consular cases and ministerial visits – it will miss out on opportunities to grow foreign investments and markets for its products. Other countries are not overlooking such opportunities.

Finally, investment in aid and development is in Australia's national interest, quite apart from the humanitarian benefits. It is in Australia's interests to invest in its neighbours' health systems to reduce the incidence and spread of infectious diseases. Or to continue to invest in Indonesia's education system when the other major funder is Saudi Arabia. In a contested and competitive region, aid is a tool of statecraft to exercise influence, whether through infrastructure development or through cooperation on common challenges such as cybersecurity, maritime security or transnational crime.

Australia's current lack of investment in diplomacy smacks of either arrogance or fatalism. It would be arrogance to suggest that Australia doesn't need to work to promote itself and convince others of its point of view. It would be fatalism to decide that we have no hope of influencing the world and that our only option is to shore up our defences. As an example of what is possible, Australia could look at Japan in the Philippines. Due to two generations of diplomatic and financial investment, Japan is now thought of not as a wartime occupier but as the Philippines' most trusted foreign partner after the United States.

To build its capacity to influence the world, Australia must properly resource its diplomatic efforts either to the levels of comparable countries or to the levels it had in the past when it faced similar geopolitical demands. Otherwise, it will fail to respond to the challenges of an uncertain future.

In his foreword to the 2017 White Paper, Prime Minister Malcolm Turnbull wrote, "We cannot assume that prosperity and security just happen by themselves." Unfortunately, the current funding of DFAT appears to assume just that.

THE RESPONSE: The minister for foreign affairs, Marise Payne, declined to comment. ■

The author is grateful to Mitchell Vandewerdt-Holman for his research assistance.

Reviews

How to Defend Australia

Hugh White

La Trobe University Press

I have always admired Hugh White for his clarity of thought, his pellucid prose and the way he "shows his work", explaining the assumptions that shape his conclusions. His latest book, *How to Defend Australia*, is true to form – seeking, as he puts it, to lay out "what risks we are trying to manage, then what role we expect armed force to play in managing them, then what kinds of operations our forces would need to undertake to perform those

roles, then what capabilities can best conduct those operations, and, finally, how they could be built and maintained, and how much they would cost".

There's no doubt that these are the right questions, and this is the time to be asking them, as Australia enters a new period of great-power confrontation. And while I do disagree with some of Professor White's answers, I found myself continually nodding in agreement with a great deal of his argument. As I am an Australian based mostly in the United States and looking back from abroad, it's perhaps unsurprising that my perspective differs somewhat from his. So let me briefly lay those differences out.

The two principal risks White identifies are the rise of China and the decline of the United States. Predicting that China will soon eclipse the United States (at least in the Western Pacific), he suggests that Australia's traditional approach of depending "on a great ally, first Britain then America, to defend us from a major attack" will no longer work. This is exactly the right way to frame the problem: China rising, American primacy fading, and therefore an increasing need for self-reliance. Yet it's far from certain that China's future will look much like its last four decades, the timeframe White chooses as a reference.

China's economy has been in a severe slowdown since about 2014, with GDP growth dipping 28 per cent per capita, or 30 per cent in real terms, against the country's post-1978 baseline. To boost its tanking economy, in 2015 Beijing launched the largest stimulus package in history – more than a trillion US dollars – but its effects have largely worn off, leaving Chinese companies deeply in debt. Cracks are appearing in the nation's credit system: at least three lending institutions have failed in the past six months. These problems pre-date the current trade war, but US tariffs have worsened them: data for July 2019 showed Chinese industrial output at a seventeen-year low.

In political and military terms, China's future is equally uncertain. Whatever the outcome of today's Hong Kong crisis, its impact on China's already limited soft power (and on prospects for peaceful reunification with Taiwan) has been dreadful, as have reports of a million Uighur Muslims languishing in re-education camps. The one-child policy has resulted in a People's Liberation Army (PLA) composed largely of only sons – "little emperors", as some Chinese call them – making China's military more casualty-averse (and more constrained by public opinion) than in the past. China may therefore have more than enough to deal with in its immediate neighbourhood for the next few decades, leaving Beijing little bandwidth to contest US pre-eminence in the Pacific.

But it's not clear that the threat from China is one against which the Australian Defence Force (ADF), either as it exists now, or in the revised configuration that White proposes, would be particularly relevant. Conventional capabilities – ships, planes and tanks – are far from central to China's "Three Warfares" strategic doctrine, which focuses on non-military means. The PLA's military modernisation is mainly intended to keep adversaries focused (and spending) on traditional warfare while China pursues its goals through other means, including cyberwarfare, political subversion, economic penetration, debt-trap diplomacy and technology theft.

It is worth noting that the

PLA's build-up over the past decade – in particular, its impressive growth in maritime, space, and air and missile capability – remains largely untested. China has fought no ground war since the Sino–Vietnamese War of 1979, no air-to-air campaign since the Korean War in the 1950s and no major naval battle since losing to the Imperial Japanese Navy on the Yalu River back in 1894. As a result, Chinese strategists are relatively risk-averse when it comes to conventional warfare, preferring pre-conflict shaping (the political, economic and cyber means mentioned earlier, along with what they call "legal warfare" and "public opinion warfare") to achieve what Sun Tzu called "the acme of skill: to subdue the enemy without fighting".

White clearly recognises this, arguing that Australia's defence force needs to be optimised for a time when attempts to deter or prevent open warfare have failed. In effect, he is suggesting that since the ADF cannot do much about Chinese pre-conflict shaping activities, we should prepare for the worst case: a maritime, air or amphibious assault on Australia's mainland, or the seizure of an outlying territory.

But I'm not convinced that this actually is the worst case. China need never contemplate such a risky venture as a major attack on or invasion of Australia when it could more easily isolate us from allies and partners in the Asia-Pacific, penetrate and subvert our economy and political system, and interdict the global links that keep our economy functioning, thereby subduing us without fighting. (Sun Tzu would surely approve.)

To take one example, Australia imports virtually all its petroleum. According to the Australian Petroleum Statistics for May 2019, 83 per cent of this comes from ten countries: in order of volume, Singapore, Malaysia, South Korea, Japan, China, the United Arab Emirates, the Netherlands, Brunei, the United States and Libya. Some of these supplies are highly vulnerable to interdiction at source; others could be disrupted en route through naval and air action, special operations, cyberattacks or economic warfare (price manipulation, strangulation of refinery supply chains) by adversaries who could thereby shut our economy down without ever approaching our shores.

Mapping the network of shipping routes, production sites and terminals through which that petroleum flows – and, not incidentally, reducing our dependence on imported petroleum – might result in a radically different set of defence priorities than focusing on protecting our coastline. Analyses of trade (exports and imports mostly move by sea) or telecommunications (we are heavily reliant on space systems and on 97,000 kilometres of undersea fibre-optic cables that land in Australia, and can be interdicted from afar) produce a similar picture, showing a country whose interests and vulnerabilities – whether in times of peace, tension short of conflict, or major war – are not synonymous with its geography.

So, it is arguable that Australia's future security depends more on our ability to influence and shape our environment short of major conflict – to build alliances with neighbours, work with coalition partners and defend our interests at a distance from our shores, rather than to mount an in-extremis defence of our territory once war breaks out. And an ADF optimised for pre-conflict shaping and deterrence-at-a-distance might look a lot like an upgraded version of what we have today: with top-tier special forces, long-range submarines, offshore surveillance platforms, an ability to mount sea–air–land expeditionary operations close to home or contribute to coalitions afield, and an air force that can deter or severely damage any attacker.

This is not to say that today's ADF is ideally suited to the task: improving cyberwarfare, missile defence, intelligence, surveillance and reconnaissance (ISR) and capabilities for countering economic and political warfare would make sense. Likewise, greater investment in diplomatic and information capabilities, foreign aid, our scientific and industrial base, and civilian intelligence agencies would be smart. It might make sense to spend more on these capabilities (which sit outside the defence budget) than on assets that would only come into play if deterrence failed and an adversary appeared offshore – by which time, given our dependence on trade and energy imports, we would already be defeated.

White acknowledges these trade-offs in an admirably clear and accessible way, while noting the larger point that, as a nation, we can only afford to spend so much on defence.

He makes a compelling case that, without a powerful and engaged US ally, we will inevitably need to spend more to ensure a comparable level of security. Like other American allies – notably in Europe, but also Japan and South Korea – Australia has had the luxury of free-riding on US extended nuclear deterrence and forward-deployed American forces since the 1950s; a weaker, less engaged Washington would mean tough choices for Canberra.

I agree entirely with White's reasoning, but from my perch here in the United States things look a little different, and the premise seems a bit shaky. Just as China's rise appears more complicated and less inevitable than White suggests, America's current strategic posture is also more complex than retreat. Donald Trump's mercurial, abrasive personality and bombastic messaging often obscure the underlying contours of American policy, which is closer to what some strategists call "offshore balancing" – where a great power works through allies, intervening only sparingly to prevent rivals dominating key areas, instead of seeking actively to dominate those areas itself – than to retrenchment or decline. Stepping back from the day-to-day tweetstorm chaos, what we are actually seeing from the United States amounts to a strategic reset.

Washington is currently pulling back from over-exposure in the Middle East (withdrawing from Syria, ending support to the war in Yemen, reducing its presence in Iraq, negotiating in Afghanistan), offloading day-to-day operations to an unlikely coalition of Israel, Jordan, Saudi Arabia and the United Arab Emirates. Trump's decision to call off a strike on Iran in June, and to ignore a series of Iranian provocations since, suggests he has little interest in yet another war in the region, instead relying on economic sanctions. The same is true for North Korea, where his administration has ignored a string of attention-seeking missile launches from Pyongyang.

Trump's friendly language towards Vladimir Putin and Kim Jong-un has been combined with sanctions on Russia and North Korea, and formal withdrawal from the Intermediate-Range Nuclear Forces Treaty (a dead letter, since Russia systematically breaches it and China, Iran and North Korea never signed it).

Trump's telegraphing of informal limits on the US security guarantee to European countries under NATO's Article 5, while formally maintaining the commitment, also suggests he is keenly aware of the risk of overcommitment, and is seeking a more sustainable posture, rather than retreat or an acceptance of geopolitical decline.

Whether Trump can carry off such a reset, or his successors continue it, are vast questions. But clearly, the picture is more complex than simply an America in decline: on the contrary, a reset now might preserve American primacy until mid-century or beyond. Combined with the uncertainties of China's rise, the strategic picture may thus be both more complex and more favourable than White's conclusions suggest.

One way to view Australia's current circumstances is through the lens of crisis: for the first time in our history, Australia's major economic partner is not our primary security partner. The prospect of China going to war with America would be utterly terrible for Australia, in human and economic terms. It's also crucial to note that China is not now, and hopefully will never be, our enemy –

and that a key goal of Australia's defence posture and diplomatic policy must be to reduce the risk of such a horrific war ever happening, a point White makes at the beginning of his book. But, for exactly the same reasons, Australia's ability to act assertively in cooperation with our neighbours and other middle powers, to play a constructive, independent role that helps reduce the regional risk of conflict, is greater than ever. This, in fact, is the central point of Professor White's argument – and I could not agree more. There's little doubt that the United States would welcome a more assertive Australia, and China would likely learn to live with it, needing us economically as much as we need them.

Everyone should read and contemplate the well-considered ideas in Hugh White's book, while also considering the kinds of capabilities Australia might need if it is to play an assertive regional role short of major war. This approach, decoupled from defence of our shores and focused instead on furthering our interests in the broader region – where they actually lie – might generate new ideas on how to defend Australia.

David Kilcullen

**The Uninhabitable
Earth: Life After
Warming**
David Wallace-Wells
Allen Lane

t is worse, much worse, than you think." So begins *The Uninhabitable Earth.* This work – eloquent, brutal and unflinching – may well become the foundational text of the global climate response, as Rachel Carson's 1962 *Silent Spring* once was for the environmental movement.

The Uninhabitable Earth builds on Wallace-Wells' July 2017 article of the same name, although the article came with the tagline "Famine, economic collapse, a sun that cooks us: what climate change could wreak – sooner than you think". Within a week of publication in *New York Magazine,* the article

became the most widely read story in the publication's history (until an excerpt from Michael Wolff's *Fire and Fury* was released). It has since been republished with annotations and debate from the scientific community. Some dismissed the article as "climate porn", while others argued about the ethics of reporting on climate scenarios based on 3°C, 4°C and even higher levels of warming. After all, how do you discuss dramatic changes to the environment and subsequent disruption to individual livelihoods and entire economies without appearing alarmist or causing panic?

However, in October 2018 – months before the full-length work was published – the Intergovernmental Panel on Climate Change released the special report *Global Warming of 1.5°C.* It found there were only twelve years (now eleven) to avert wide-ranging and irreversible climate impacts that will create regional imbalances, constrain economic development and increase global inequality. The IPCC's report – the world's premier example of international peer-reviewed science – definitively states that these dangers will follow warming above 1.5°C.

Wallace-Wells's argument – of a kind with that of Swedish climate activist Greta Thunberg – is that it is now rational to be alarmed. Think how we have moved our own thin red lines. In 1997, in the Kyoto Protocol, 2°C warming was considered catastrophic, but by 2016, in the Paris Agreement, 2°C warming had become an aspirational goal. Today, only Morocco and The Gambia have targets compatible with a world 1.5°C warmer. So we are on track to shoot past 2°C. This means that actively considering the impacts of warming that is higher – as Wallace-Wells does – is now required.

Wallace-Wells lays out a smorgasbord of potential climate futures that may occur in our region and to our trading partners. He outlines "elements of chaos" that will result – heat death, hunger, drowning, wildfire, human-made disaster events, freshwater drain, dying oceans, unbreathable air, economic collapse and climate-induced conflict. These chapters are difficult reading. But they explain what must be planned for.

And plan we must. Wallace-Wells asks the reader to consider what to do if Jakarta – a metropolis

of ten million people – becomes uninhabitable due to sea level rise. In August 2019 this moved from hypothetical to reality, when Indonesia announced the government will move the capital from Jakarta to Borneo because Jakarta is sinking into the Java Sea. This moves the seat of power, but not the people. If Jakarta sinks, what will Indonesia ask of Australia? How will we respond? What other countries will step in, and how will their actions alter regional alliances? We also can't consider our response only to Jakarta, as the twenty most likely cities to be affected by sea level rise are in Asia. Who will we prioritise if Shanghai and Hong Kong and Kolkata all flood?

The Uninhabitable Earth explores the scale of expected migration in our region in the coming decades. The conservative estimate of climate refugees from Bangladesh alone is 10 million. These numbers are not a fantasy. The World Bank predicts that 140 million refugees will be displaced by climate by 2050. And that is a *conservative* estimate.

We also need to plan for countries in our region losing land. Territory and the ability to control the land within it are at the heart of the Westphalian concept of the state. Nations – and their neighbours – will cope with loss of land in unpredictable ways. Wallace-Wells notes that one reason (others include, of course, the strategic positioning of military bases to control the South China Sea) China is building artificial islands in the South China Sea is to position itself for a land-constrained future. Antarctica presents a different challenge. We have all seen images of melting glaciers and runaway icebergs. But what will Australia's security look like if the polar caps melt and Antarctica becomes an inhabitable land mass to our south?

Wallace-Wells notes that for every half-degree of warming, societies experience a 10 to 20 per cent increase in the likelihood of armed conflict. He uses Syria as a case study, drawing the link between water scarcity, a collapse in agriculture and a devastated economy that laid the conditions for the first "climate war".

This is the value of *The Uninhabitable Earth*. It presents scenarios based on different degrees of warming and asks us to consider what these mean for our politics, our economics and our very near future.

Wallace-Wells avoids the traditional – and rather opaque – language of climate change. Instead of relying on figures that are meaningless to the non-scientist (do you know what "400 parts per million" means? Or understand the difference between hitting 2°C in 2040 or 2050?), he cuts through to the personal. The possible futures he outlines may happen before the reader has paid off their mortgage and in the lifetimes of our sitting judges. This approach to speaking about our climate challenges could help shift the way governments frame policy and talk to the public.

The danger for decision-makers is to dismiss these futures as fantasy, rather than to take them seriously and prepare. Climate change is not the domain of only one department or think tank. It is not an "environmental issue". Its impacts are not a legacy of 200 years of industrialisation, but a result of the staggering increase in emissions this century. The science is clear: the majority of emissions have occurred "since Al Gore published his first book on climate" (in 1992). In other words, on the watch of many still in positions of power today.

What does a world 3°C warmer mean for Australia? *The Uninhabitable Earth* is not a policy manual, and it does not offer a "fix". But it demonstrates the need to reshape our policy in areas such as energy, defence, agriculture, infrastructure, health and trade. Wallace-Wells singles out Australia as the "test case" for "how the world's affluent societies will bend or break or rebuild". Australia is, after all, the wealthiest of the countries likely to experience climate impacts first. Our successes and failures are being watched.

This work should be required reading for all Australian decision-makers. The tyranny of distance is not enough to enable this country to ignore a warmer world. Our economy and security are at risk, as is the stability of the region. In Australia we can already smell the smoke and feel the warmth, even if the blaze itself is just out of sight.

Astrid Edwards

Race, Islam and Power: Ethnic and Religious Violence in Post-Suharto Indonesia
Andreas Harsono
Monash University Publishing

Lead singer of rock band Slank, shirt unbuttoned, wearing a red bandana, gripped his microphone and belted out ballads onstage. Ulama, religious scholars, in Middle Eastern attire paced in the wings like harried producers. On the roof a _pawang hujan_, rain shaman, warded off thunderstorms. And the crowd overfilling the 80,000-seat Gelora Bung Karno, Jakarta's biggest stadium, began a series of Mexican waves. Hands flew into the air: of _santri_ Muslims in white caps and Chinese Indonesians, people from the Javanese hinterland and islands far to the east, all singing along while waving red-and-white Indonesian flags. It seemed, in the moment, like an inspired demonstration of inclusive nationalism.

We were waiting for President Joko Widodo – Jokowi, as he is popularly known.

I asked the guy next to me why he liked Jokowi enough to come to this, his final, largest election rally, and he said because Jokowi stood for everyone: Indonesians of all races and religions.

This idea, that support for the president equates to support for diversity and tolerance, continues to be widely voiced in Indonesia – even as during his presidency Jokowi has struggled to apply such values, and sometimes has appeared to waver in his commitment to them.

I thought of Jokowi's April 2019 rally while reading Andreas Harsono's _Race, Islam and Power_. Harsono, who works for international NGO Human Rights Watch, recounts his travels across Indonesia examining past and present racial and religious violence. The narrative is structured by island, as Harsono moves from west to east, from Sumatra to Kalimantan, Java,

Maluku, Timor and then Papua, although the material comes not from a single trip but from many, taken over two decades. Riding in speedboats and SUVs to remote villages, sitting in restaurants or coffee shops in provincial cities, he speaks to victims and perpetrators, activists and politicians.

Multiracial, multireligious, multilingual Indonesia is one of many nations where intolerant forms of nationalism are currently strengthening. In such a sprawling archipelago it is crucial to manage difference adeptly. This is a nation where some citizens take boats to the Philippines to shop for groceries while fishing vessels accidentally drift into Australian waters, where some see themselves as living on Mecca's "verandah" and others identify as Melanesians. Policy must be flexible and fair; clumsy efforts at homogenisation must be avoided.

Yet the patterns of violence Harsono describes are sadly familiar, and not limited to Indonesia.In mixed, culturally diverse communities, discontent begins to fester: over distribution of wealth and political power, or demographic or cultural changes, real or perceived. Schisms run along ethnic or religious lines, grievances channelled into a scapegoated "other". Then comes political or economic turbulence. Rumours spread, fear takes over, and militias, insurrections or mobs form. Afterwards, survivors of the violence attempt to rebuild their lives, often while living in the same neighbourhoods as their persecutors. In Kalimantan, Indonesian Borneo, Harsono speaks to a widow raising a daughter who does not know of her mixed ancestry or her father's murder – both are kept secret for her own good, he is told.

Cynical political manipulation or direct state involvement often fuels such tragedies. In Indonesia, the largest-scale perpetrator of such tactics was former president Suharto's New Order regime. Despite the book's subtitle of "Ethnic and Religious Violence in Post-Suharto Indonesia", much of the text discusses Suharto's and his predecessor Sukarno's roles in kindling ethnic and religious tensions. Harsono remarks that in 1945 Indonesia's first social democratic prime minister, Sutan Syahrir, warned about militarist elements – "our own fascists" – waiting to take control of the new nation, a prescience realised with the rise of the New Order.

A rigid conception of Indonesian nationalism, Harsono argues, has been a stimulus for tensions. The political class has long failed to counter perceptions that the country is run by and for Java. Instead of addressing regional grievances, Jakarta has often tried to enforce homogenising "pro-Indonesia" fidelities. In Aceh, Harsono finds civil servants forced to take oaths of loyalty and participate in mandated ceremonies to raise Indonesia's flag. In Timor, his observations lead to stark conclusions – the "Jakarta elite", he notes acerbically, lack not just the "intellectual prowess" but the "imagination" to manage Indonesia.

Sukarno's formation of a unitary Indonesian state in 1950, superseding a looser federation, helped fuel conflict between a dominant centre and indignant regions. Yet exclusivist, majoritarian politics have also been practised at local and provincial levels, including by Christians in Christian-majority areas. The decentralisation of political power following the New Order created more opportunities

for such behaviour: mayors and governors could build political support by practising ethnic or religious favouritism over jobs and funding. Aceh, granted special autonomy, began using an interpretation of sharia law to punish religious minorities, women, gay and transgender people; its example has inspired other provincial and local governments.

Charting the recent increase in religious intolerance, Harsono shares the common view that Susilo Bambang Yudhoyono's presidency was disastrous. Under Yudhoyono, local "consultation" was allowed over religious matters, leading to widespread closures of houses of worship for minority religions. Islamic groups were permitted to pursue the Ahmadiyya community, whom they consider a "deviant sect", and were thereby emboldened. A blasphemy law, previously rarely applied, began to be wielded aggressively.

Race, Islam and Power has had a long gestation: most of Harsono's travel occurred between 2003 and 2006. Today, conservative religious identities are influencing politics more prominently, and discrimination and harassment are rising. Yet large-scale violence of the kind that much of the book describes – roughly 10,000 people died in Maluku in Christian–Muslim violence in 1999 and 2000, for example – has declined. By that low bar, there has been progress.

Harsono sees uneven rates of development, and particularly neglect of eastern Indonesia, as a cause of tensions throughout the country's history. Jokowi has promised to address this, and has indeed launched major infrastructure projects in the outer islands. Papua, though, remains deeply troubled. A culture of military impunity continues. Jokowi has also been passive on majoritarian religious laws. While this passivity is an improvement over Yudhoyono, overall he has shown little willingness to spend political capital fighting intolerance.

Harsono argues that the answers to Indonesia's recurrent racial and religious violence lie in robust human rights protection and civil liberties, multicultural policies and the allowance of "multiple identities", environmental protection and better stewardship and sharing of resources, and secular nationalism grounded in equality and mutual respect. While Jokowi at times pledges support for some of these goals, his strategy appears to be more about muddling through. In and beyond his second term, if the country can avoid flare-ups on the scale of the 2016–2017 anti-Ahok protests, and political stability and economic growth are maintained, the comforts of exclusive identities, and resentments and fears of various "others", might fade.

At Gelora Bung Karno Stadium, Jokowi said Indonesia consisted of many races and religions; he listed provinces and islands, asked if people from those areas were in the house, greeted them in their regional languages. He said Islam could not be the basis of the Indonesian state, that the foundation philosophy Pancasila, which specifies belief in God, was "final". Then he talked of his program – infrastructure, human capital – while evoking grand national aspirations: that Indonesia *maju* (advance) and become a *negara besar* (major power). Vice-presidential candidate Maruf Amin – one of the country's most powerful clerics, and a staunch conservative –

then led an Arabic-studded prayer. I found myself watching Grace Natalie, Chinese Christian leader of a new progressive party, as she stood behind Maruf and participated in it.

There was no reckoning with Indonesia's history, and no blueprint for resolving current tensions within the archipelago. Without recognition of the often divergent perspectives and interests across regions, Jokowi's listing of places and inclusive greetings looked like tokenism. And what attitude to diversity was signalled by making the multi-faith crowd stand compliant as Maruf, who has hounded minorities with fatwas, prayed?

Jokowi and Maruf were the rally's intended climax. Yet the crowd followed its own rhythm. During Jokowi's speech many were less engaged than they'd been before it. Streams of people left their seats; others chatted. Perhaps the pre-Jokowi entertainment – a visibly diverse band of pop stars, brought together to sing of the right all *rakyat jelata*, ordinary folk, have to dignity – more crisply articulated their reason for supporting Jokowi's presidency than anything he actually had to say. Many kept standing and cheering after Jokowi had left the stage. Perhaps they were waiting for something else, or were imagining it themselves – some more fundamental recasting of one-size-fits-all nationalism, some firm plan to undertake recognitions and reconciliations, some step beyond "tolerance" as mere maintenance of civil peace. A genuine commitment to the pluralism they could see, at Gelora Bung Karno, all around them.

David Fettling

**Peak Japan: The End
of Great Ambitions**
Brad Glosserman
Georgetown University
Press/Footprint Books

As the waves of confusion and horror from Japan's Fukushima nuclear disaster and tsunami swept across the country on 11 March 2011, I spent the evening at a small official Japanese dinner. This meant that, ironically, on that night at least, I gained a better insight into the forces of stasis at work in modern Japan than the author of this important new book himself did. Such was the need to follow diplomatic protocol that there was no abandonment of the dinner program to catch up with the news on television, or even a break for a collective smartphone update – although some guests could not resist doing that surreptitiously.

Brad Glosserman watched the disaster unfold from a California hotel room. "It was a spellbinding experience," he recalls in *Peak Japan*, particularly because, as a long-time watcher of the nation, he began to ponder immediately whether this was a "Meiji moment".

That phrase refers to the way Japan suddenly re-entered global politics in the late nineteenth century – after two centuries of isolation under the shōguns – when some far-sighted thinkers used the restoration of the Meiji emperor to turn the country into a modern industrial and military power. Depending on one's ideological taste or sense of history, there have been other such moments since. The rise of the fanatical military state in the 1930s, the remarkable economic recovery after World War II and development into an innovative export powerhouse, and that tantalising point in the late 1980s when some analysts thought the booming Japanese economy would overtake the United States' in size all come to mind.

In the years since the financial bust of 1989, Japanophiles, not least this one, have often grasped at various events to identify a new Meiji moment. There will be a lot of it going on in the next twelve months as Shinzō Abe becomes the country's longest-serving prime minister and the Olympic Games return to Tokyo for the first time since 1964. But Glosserman is having none of this. Through the regret-tinged lens of someone who has spent his career engaged with Japan, he argues that these events will simply mark the arrival of "Peak Japan", from which there is likely nowhere to go but down.

Glosserman concedes this thesis won't be popular. That will be true in Australia, where much of our Indo-Pacific strategy has been built around the rapid advance of our military ties with Japan over the past decade. And Japan is central to Australia's new challenge of managing China's regional infrastructure ambitions. Glosserman writes: "For Japan's allies and partners, Peak Japan undercuts fundamental assumptions about order in Asia and the wider Asia-Pacific region. Anyone with an interest in Asian regional dynamics should be concerned about a gap between expectations of Japan and what the country can and will deliver."

The book was inspired by Japan's messy management of the Fukushima disaster, but is also built on an analysis of how the country failed to rise to the challenge of three less dramatic but equally significant shocks this century. They are the 2008 global financial crisis; the 2009 election victory of the leftish Democratic Party of Japan, which marked the first time voters cleanly removed the Liberal Democratic Party from office since 1955; and the 2010 territorial dispute with China over islands in the East China Sea. Then he turns to Abe's return to office in 2012, which ushered in his eponymous Abenomics reforms designed to stimulate the economy and make Japan more competitive. This development is left hanging as a shock in the making but more likely was the beginning of "Peak Japan".

Glosserman is not writing off Japan – especially while Abe remains in control – noting that it will continue to be a major player in diplomacy, business and technology. And the government is starting to negotiate the key challenges the country faces, such as an ageing population. But, he writes, "the sense of alarm, even with trigger events such as the four shocks, is not sufficient to move the Japanese people out of their comfort zone and to change direction from business as usual ... the pace of change is insufficient to overcome the larger forces at work, and as a result, Japan can no longer harbor grand ambitions".

To recap, Japan's challenges include: a declining population due to low fertility and low immigration; an anaemic economy where a deflationary mindset has taken root; an underfunded health and aged-care system; wasteful fiscal stimulus packages that have led to the highest debt-to-GDP ratio in the world; declining voter participation in elections; a foreign policy stalemate between a nationalist governing elite and a citizenry with a pacifist mindset; and an increasingly insular and celibate younger generation.

The most interesting narrative that flows through *Peak Japan* involves the exhaustive detailing of how many substantial government and independent studies have been conducted over the past three decades into these and other challenges, including the Fukushima disaster. Despite its reputation

for a "see no evil" consensus approach to public policy, Japan has arguably analysed its condition and outlook more exhaustively than any country in the world. Yet "the national trajectory remains largely unaltered", Glosserman tells us.

Glosserman doesn't provide a simple, compelling explanation for Japan's failure to act. At times he says it is simply inexplicable. He also puts it down to elements such as a deep sense of pride in a distinctive socio-economic model that values process over change. When he digs deeper into culture, he finds that while most Japanese deeply value *wa* (harmony) and *kizuna* (social bonds), these concepts are viewed differently by the right and the left in modern Japan, creating a roadblock to any sort of national rebirth.

Abe's remarkable longevity in office and activism abroad have papered over these more fundamental issues at home. The July 2019 election for the country's upper house was a case in point. It was Abe's sixth election victory since returning to office in 2012 – a testament to his campaigning skills. But the voter turnout was the second-lowest on record –

a testament to the public's sense of disengagement from the real long-term challenges.

One of the distinctive features of the Meiji Restoration was how Japan shed its Asian identity in certain ways to become the equal of Western powers. A key test for Peak Japan will be how this less ambitious, more constrained country finds a new identity among the dynamic rising countries in the region. This will be important for Australia's foreign policy. While China is the obvious country to watch, the downturn in relations with South Korea in 2019 over colonial-era grievances show this is yet another serious challenge that will require some new thinking by Japan.

Japan still matters. In a world increasingly focused on the Thucydides Trap implications of declining US power, Glosserman reminds us of another transition – less destabilising but fascinating nonetheless.

Greg Earl

Correspondence

"In Denial" by
Hugh White

Jonathan Pryke

Hugh White's article "In Denial" (AFA6: *Our Sphere of Influence*) is both interesting and provocative.

It is interesting because White explains Australia's strategic anxiety in relation to our immediate region, and why China might be interested in setting up a military base in the Pacific, better than anyone else I have read.

It is provocative because he calls for Australia to abandon its ambition of retaining an "exclusive sphere of influence". He argues that "[t]he costs to us of trying to keep China out of the region might simply prove impossible to bear" and that nothing we are doing to counter China's ambitions "seems to be working". This is where his argument falters.

To explain why, we need to take a step back and look at China's growing presence in the region in a bit more detail. Significant pockets of ethnic Chinese have resided in the Pacific for more than a century. For example, the second prime minister of Papua New Guinea, Julius Chan, still a member of parliament, is partly ethnic Chinese. On top of that, the China–Taiwan tension continues to play out in the region, as six of Taiwan's remaining nineteen diplomatic allies are based there. This has led to some degree of engagement from both sides.

Since 2006, however, Chinese activity in the Pacific has dramatically increased. Whereas twenty years ago the most common foreign face that a Pacific islander would see in their nation would be from Australia, New Zealand or the United States, now it is most certainly Chinese. Chinese state-owned enterprises and infrastructure projects litter every major Beijing-supporting capital, and Chinese stores trade in every large town. The seeds of this engagement have been fuelled by Chinese aid.

Given this footprint on the ground, you would be forgiven for thinking that China has become the largest benefactor in the Pacific. Data from the Lowy Institute Pacific Aid Map, however, shows that between 2011 and 2016 China, the third-largest aid donor, invested only 8 per cent of all aid flows to the Pacific. Australia contributed 45 per cent, followed by New Zealand, with 9 per cent. China has a long way to go to overtake Australia.

On top of that, since 2016 Chinese aid to the Pacific has been in relative decline. This is largely thanks to nations in the region being less open to China's costly infrastructure projects, backed by debt and implemented by Chinese companies.

For the most part, China's engagement in the region has not been driven by some overarching grand strategy. It's far messier than that. Much of the engagement has been driven by Chinese state-owned enterprises. These are mandated to export surplus labour and capital, while at the same time they seek to make a profit for themselves far from the prying eye of Beijing. Labourers who arrived with these projects, or who came through family links or fishing vessels, discovered high-cost economies and stayed. A trade store in Funafuti, Tuvalu, can make you a lot more money than one in Fujian, China. These groups quickly put down roots, without any significant diplomatic support. To give China some credit, it has also charmed elites in the Pacific with the red-carpet treatment in Beijing – a practice Australia is now emulating.

While China's influence in the region has been growing from the bottom up, it has been developing a strategy in recent years to take advantage of its newfound leverage. Western capitals have become convinced that China is now eager to set up a military base somewhere in the Pacific, for reasons White so eloquently lays out.

I have yet to see, however, anything that shows me that China's ambition in the region goes any further than strategic opportunism. From China's perspective, the Pacific represents a relatively low-cost gamble for a potentially large win. But how much is China willing to actually stump up to disrupt the status quo in the Pacific?

Prime Minister Scott Morrison's "Pacific step-up" shows Australia's resolve. Building on an already solid base – Australia's investment has never been wanting, though our attention often has – Morrison is devoting more time and money to the region. The step-up is not about establishing an "exclusive sphere of influence" (something we have never had in the Pacific), but it is about retaining Australia's position as the partner of choice, and responding to any strategic ambition of China's that threatens our national interest.

So far, while climate change is preventing Australia from forming strong partnerships with some, the step-up is succeeding. Morrison's personal charm offensive deserves credit for this – five Pacific visits in a year is more than most prime ministers would make in their entire tenure.

But it is succeeding in large part thanks to the Pacific islands themselves. Leaders of these nations have expressed time and again that they have no interest in the region being further militarised – by Australia or by China. They have been alert to the challenges of China's engagement longer than Australia has. Now that Australia has woken up, our renewed attention, aligned with the interests of Pacific leaders, shows China that they will have to be more than opportunistic in their engagement in the Pacific.

The threat of China setting up a military base in the Pacific is serious. But it is one that, thanks to Australian vigilance and an alignment of interests with our Pacific friends, can and should be managed. Now is not the time for strategic fatalism.

Jonathan Pryke is director of the Pacific Islands Program at the Lowy Institute

Wesley Morgan

n his brutally honest assessment, Hugh White is right to suggest that the one constant in Australia's approach to the Pacific has been the strategic imperative of denying the islands to other powers. In the early 1950s a senior official in the Department of External Affairs, R.N. Hamilton, described the aim of Australia's Pacific policy as "to exert dominant political influence in the area with a view to maintaining Australian security behind a peripheral screen of islands". We would be hard-pressed to find a better description of the motivations behind Australia's current "step-up" in the Pacific, which is driven by concern about the increasing influence of a powerful and worryingly authoritarian China. However, the region has changed greatly since the 1950s, with the emergence of no less than fourteen new island nations.

White is also right to suggest that Australia "should start to treat our smaller close neighbours as independent at last". It may seem paradoxical but relinquishing crude attempts to exercise a veto over the foreign policy of island states would almost certainly help Australia to maintain its influence in the region. Pacific leaders have long resented Canberra's tendency to pay attention only when its strategic anxieties are roused. It reminds them that in Australian eyes, Pacific island states don't matter in their own right. Yet they do matter on the international stage. Far from being powerless, these island nations are significant actors in global politics. They form an important voting bloc at the United Nations and are sovereign over a large swathe of the Earth's surface. Against significant opposition from powerful countries, at times including the United States, Japan and France, they have successfully pursued their interests: they have secured recognition of their exclusive economic zones under the Law of the Sea treaty, banned driftnet fishing in the South Pacific, negotiated a regional treaty for American boats fishing in their waters, and had New Caledonia and French Polynesia added to the United Nations' list of non-self-governing territories. Today, island leaders have endorsed a Blue Pacific strategy to work together as an ocean continent to pursue shared interests.

Australia should strengthen its relationship with Pacific island states not for the narrow purpose of competing with China, but because durable relations with neighbouring states are in Australia's national interest. White is again correct when he writes that the proposed Australian naval base in Papua New Guinea is likely a bit of flag-waving, and that when it comes to infrastructure spending China has much deeper pockets. Australia would struggle to compete for influence on those terms. However, White underplays other aspects of Australia's relationship with the Pacific, in the form of people-to-people links, migration, labour mobility and education. For example, Canberra could readily improve relations, and derive economic benefits, by creating more accessible pathways for Pacific islanders to work and study in Australia.

As White suggests, there is clearly a mismatch between the strategic priorities of Australia and those of Pacific island countries. These nations tend to view China differently from Australia. Pacific leaders point out that the threats posed by a more powerful China are potentialities. By contrast, they know climate change is happening, and that its impacts – stronger cyclones, devastating floods, rising seas, dying reefs and ocean acidification – will become worse the longer the world fails to curb emissions.

White's analysis falls down in its failure to engage properly with climate change. His experience and background are in analysing security threats of a certain kind: hard power conflict, wars between states, threats at the border. He is not alone in this regard. Australia's strategic and defence community struggles to appreciate the profound threat posed by a changing climate.

Security analysts ought to be able to help with devising a response to climate change. In their work they forecast scenarios, weigh up risks, provide advice to government about where to invest resources, and detail strategies for dealing with incipient threats. Tackling climate change requires exactly these skill sets. What is needed is an investment in diplomacy and statecraft, to reinforce global rules intended to reduce emissions. Pacific island countries are way ahead of Australia in this regard; they have shaped the global climate regime for decades. They were crucial to the negotiation of the 2015 Paris Agreement, which is, despite its flaws, the only multilateral mechanism we have to avoid cataclysmic changes to our planet. Pacific states are calling on all nations to abide by Paris Agreement commitments, and they look especially to Australia. There is little doubt that Canberra's continued failure to reduce emissions, or to move away from coal-fired power, is undercutting its influence in the region.

Australia should see Pacific island states not as potential sources of threat in its patch, but as partners. If Australia wants to strengthen the rules-based global order in ways that protect its interests, Pacific island states would prove powerful allies, not liabilities. Australia need only learn to listen.

Wesley Morgan is a lecturer at the University of the South Pacific in Fiji and an adjunct fellow at Griffith Asia Institute

Hugh White responds

Thanks to Jonathan Pryke and Wesley Morgan for their thoughtful responses to my essay. Both raise important issues that touch on how we see China, how we see the South Pacific and how we see ourselves.

Let's start with how we see China. Jonathan Pryke suggests that I am too pessimistic about our chances to preserve our sphere of influence in the South Pacific, in part because I overestimate China's resolve to challenge it. He notes that so far China's efforts to build its regional role in our backyard have been modest, uncoordinated and without clear strategic intent.

But policymaking is all about shaping the future, so the question we should ask is whether this is likely to remain so in the decades to come. This is where the reports of China's interest in establishing a military presence, which the Australian government takes so seriously, enter the picture. The reports indicate that China plans a very different kind of engagement in future – one that is much more "strategic", in both senses.

That is precisely the evidence of China's ambition that Pryke says he has yet to see. Of course, we are not in a position to evaluate the information on which this assessment is based – and claims about a proposed Chinese base in Vanuatu were widely denied – but it seems unwise to assume that the government has got its concerns about China's intentions in the South Pacific wrong. That is especially so when the assessment is consistent, as I think it is, with judgements about China's strategic objectives in the wider region.

As I argue in the essay, challenging Australia's claim to primacy in our sub-region fits China's ambition to establish itself as the dominant power in East Asia and the Western Pacific. China is willing to commit a great deal to achieving that ambition, which is why I do not share Pryke's doubts that China is willing to "stump up to disrupt the status quo in the [South] Pacific".

We should be careful not to repeat our past mistakes here. It is now more than twenty-five years since Australian governments started to think about the strategic implications of China's rise, and we have consistently underestimated both its power and its resolve. We have tended to assume that it could never match America economically or challenge it militarily in Asia, and that it would never have the courage to contest the region's US-led order.

It was a classic extrapolation error, and only now, decades after the evidence has become unmistakable, have we woken up to the fact that China might in future look and act very differently from the way it has in the past. We should bear that in mind in extrapolating from China's past in the South Pacific to the decades ahead.

Prkye also thinks I am too pessimistic about the quality of Australia's response to the challenge that China poses to our position in the South Pacific. He is much more impressed by the prime minister's "Pacific step-up" than I am. I agree that Scott Morrison's frequent visits are a welcome change from the more usual pattern of neglect, but there is scant evidence that they have done much to strengthen Australia's regional standing.

It partly depends on the balance between charm and offence in the prime minister's "charm offensive", and the jury must be out on that after the awkward atmospherics of this year's Pacific Islands Forum summit in Tuvalu. But more importantly, to take "an alignment of interests with our South Pacific friends" for granted, as Pryke seems to do, is to assume precisely what needs to be established. It is far from clear that our South Pacific friends will see their interests aligning with ours more readily than with China's in the decades to come.

Wesley Morgan makes the excellent point that the best way to build that alignment of interests might well be not to focus on China and its role, but to concentrate on tending to our own relationships with our neighbours. Almost sixty years since they began to gain independence, it is time to rethink how best to do that, and move away from the aid-driven model which has, it seems, served us rather poorly. I agree with Morgan when he argues that we should focus on building closer, deeper people-to-people links. He lists migration, education and labour mobility, and he is absolutely right. If the Pacific step-up is to amount to anything more than a passing piece of political packaging, it must focus on substantial initiatives in these areas.

And that leaves climate change. It was clear before Tuvalu that this is a big problem for Morrison's Pacific policy, and it is even clearer since the summit. As Morgan fairly points out, this is not my field, but I take the issue very seriously. I am not sure he's right that we strategy and defence types have much to contribute to better climate policy – just look at the mess we have made of defence policy in recent decades. But more broadly, Australia's climate policy has not faltered through lack of analysis, but through failure of political leadership, on all sides.

It need hardly be said that the consequences of this failure go far beyond the problems it causes for our influence in the South Pacific. Indeed, important though the South Pacific is to Australia, it pales into insignificance compared with the kind of climate shifts that now seem probable and the effects this will have on our national life. So it seems a little disingenuous to use the problems of Pacific diplomacy as an argument for better climate policy when much bigger issues of the habitability of our continent and planet are on the table. Maybe that's part of what our neighbours were trying to tell our prime minister in Tuvalu: climate change is not just their problem, but ours.

Hugh White is an emeritus professor of strategic studies
at the Australian National University

Correspondence

"Cross Purposes" by
Jenny Hayward-Jones

Sandra Tarte

I n the subtitle of her essay for "Cross Purposes" (AFA6: *Our Sphere of Influence*), Jenny Hayward-Jones poses the question "why is Australia's Pacific influence waning?" This is a compelling query for a country that has for so long enjoyed a position of dominance and leadership in the region. And it has underpinned Australia's diplomatic push into the Pacific to reclaim (or retain) the position of partner of choice – whether in the development, security or political sphere.

For the first time in the postcolonial era, Australia has found itself competing with an alternative regional power in China. This contest is having some positive spin-offs for Pacific nations as they are presented with new offers of support and new avenues for development. But there is also the possibility of a dangerous escalation of tensions reminiscent of the Cold War. Australia is projecting its anxieties and concerns about China onto the Pacific and allowing its regional policies to be shaped by this lens.

The competitive dynamic also creates a false dichotomy, implying that there is a choice for Pacific nations between two rival partners. The reality is that Pacific countries need Australia, just as Australia needs them. Ultimately those in the region need Australia to "step up" on climate action and must find ways to influence Canberra on its number-one security priority. So, in addition to examining Australia's diplomatic approach, as Hayward-Jones does in her essay, it is also necessary to examine the Pacific's diplomatic approach to Australia.

In recent years there has been a trend among Pacific nations towards playing a more assertive role in regional and global affairs. As former Kiribati president Anote Tong stated bluntly in 2012: "We have no choice but to engage even more aggressively internationally because the key to our survival will depend on whether international action is taken on climate change." This has led to more proactive diplomacy, and has seen the influence of the island states, collectively and individually, rise on the global stage. But this newfound confidence among Pacific nations in declaring and asserting their interests will ultimately be meaningless unless "the climate rift", as Hayward-Jones terms it, between Australia and the Pacific region is somehow bridged.

The Forty-Ninth Pacific Islands Forum (PIF), held in 2018, was significant as it was the first time that Australia was unable to water down the language of the forum's communiqué on climate change. As Hayward-Jones notes, it signed on to a declaration that recognised climate change as the region's "single greatest threat to livelihoods, security and well-being". Australia faced an even stronger declaration in Tuvalu at the 2019 PIF leaders' summit, which it was only partially able to deflect and water down. This underscores an important synergy (but also tension) in Pacific diplomacy. Australia has long used its membership of the PIF to influence, if not manage, regional affairs in line with its own interests. But a key reason that Pacific island nations invited Australia and New Zealand into the forum was to influence these former metropolitan powers, particularly on trade and development issues. As one of its founding fathers, Fiji's first prime minister, Ratu Sir Kamisese Mara, argued: "We were happy to be joined by Australia and New Zealand ... for part of the ambitious plan of the Forum ... was no less than to alter the whole balance of the terms of trade."

The perception that Australia and New Zealand exerted "undue influence" over the PIF eventually fuelled some Pacific countries to form alternative regional institutions. It also led to calls – most notably by Fiji's prime minister Frank Bainimarama – for Australia and New Zealand to be excluded from the PIF. Those calls were echoed at the end of the Tuvalu PIF leaders' summit. But Fiji is back in the forum's fold, and the opportunity has returned for member states to again use it to influence its largest member on the policies that matter most. With Australia on board, the region will be better positioned to take on other major carbon polluters, including China.

Almost thirty-five years ago, forum leaders in their communiqué noted China's "strong interest in playing a helpful and constructive role in the region".

They also noted "Australia's offer to facilitate productive contacts" between China and the region. Obviously, threat perceptions can and do change. For the Pacific, climate change is already viewed as an existential threat to vulnerable low-lying islands. But this is not just a problem for the Pacific islands. The challenge Australia sees from a rising China may well pale in comparison to the coming climate crisis. It is therefore time for the PIF to frame climate change more broadly, as an existential threat to all its members – Australia included.

Sandra Tarte is associate professor and head of the School of Government, Development and International Affairs at the University of the South Pacific

Paul Ronalds

Jenny Hayward-Jones is right to call out the inconsistency on climate change at the heart of the Australian government's "step-up" in the Pacific. For Pacific islanders, climate change is an existential threat. This was made clear to me on a visit to Taro Island, in the Choiseul Province of Solomon Islands, a few years ago.

Satellite data suggests sea levels in the Solomon Islands are rising up to five times faster than the global average, at 7.7 millimetres per year in the capital of Honiara, which lies to the south of the country, and up to 16.8 millimetres a year in the north, where Taro Island is located. As a result, Taro Island is expected to be the first provincial capital in the world to be abandoned due to climate change. Most of the island is less than 2 metres above sea level and, with the high probability of tsunamis from the constant seismic activity, it's simply not safe.

In Australia, on the other hand, members of the government continue to advocate for coal-fired power stations. The latest evidence suggests Australia is not on track to achieve its Paris Agreement targets.

Unfortunately, this is just one of a number of areas where there is a lack of coherence in Australia's foreign and domestic policies towards the Pacific. Many of these involve its aid program.

As Hayward-Jones points out, Australia's aid has for many years focused on improving governance and strengthening state institutions. However, Australia's domestic priorities have often undermined these goals. The decision to re-establish offshore processing of refugees on Manus Island is a prime example. Kevin Rudd's deal with former Papua New Guinea prime minister Peter O'Neill to reopen a Manus Island refugee detention facility crippled Australia's ability to raise growing concerns about corruption during O'Neill's tenure. It also distorted Australia's aid program. A key part of the deal was a $200 million commitment to a new hospital in Lae. This commitment effectively put on hold other projects until the cash could be found. There are far more cost-effective ways to improve health outcomes (including building low-cost provincial clinics) in a country where the biggest causes of childhood deaths are easily preventable conditions such as pneumonia, diarrhoea, measles and malaria.

In contrast, the government's recent decision to invest $13 million in fighting tuberculosis in the Pacific and $10 million in combating the recent outbreak of polio in Papua New Guinea are excellent examples of health investments likely to produce high development returns, and where our national interests and those of our Pacific neighbours are deeply intertwined. At the closest point, there is only around four kilometres between Papua New Guinea and the Torres Strait Islands, a relatively short distance for drug-resistant tuberculosis to cross.

Australia also has a significant interest in promoting economic growth in our region, but whether we have chosen the most cost-effective interventions is debatable.

Scott Morrison's proposed Australian Infrastructure Financing Facility for the Pacific includes a $2 billion mix of grants and loans to support economic growth. Of this, $500 million will come from the aid budget. There is no doubt that the Pacific needs investment in infrastructure. However, almost one in two children in Papua New Guinea have stunted growth due to chronic malnutrition, which is the fourth-highest rate in the world. This poses a major threat to sustainable economic growth in the nation. Save the Children's 2017 report, *Short Changed*, estimates that child undernutrition costs the Papua New Guinean economy between 2.81 per cent and a staggering 8.41 per cent of its annual gross domestic product through reduced earning capacity, household income and productivity. Similarly, a multi-agency report published in June 2019, *Unseen, Unsafe*, highlights the massive economic cost of endemic levels of violence against children. If the Australian government is looking for a cost-effective investment in the region's most important asset, its people, to spur long-term growth, it could start by addressing malnutrition or violence.

Another area of poor policy coherence is labour mobility. Julie Bishop's championing of the Pacific Labour Scheme while foreign minister was very welcome. However, rather than integrating our foreign policy goals in the region with domestic policy settings, we have allowed four times as many backpackers (from non-Pacific nations) to work in Australia as seasonal workers.

There are many other examples.

Prime Minister Morrison's diplomatic visits to the region are a great signal. So too is his use of the language of family to characterise the kind of relationship that Australia wants to have with its closest neighbours. However, to give real meaning to this, Australia will need to make domestic policy choices that support the Pacific step-up's objectives, especially when it comes to the greatest threat to the region, climate change.

Ultimately, if Australia wants to be influential in the Pacific it will need to ensure all of its foreign policy tools are being used to promote the step-up – aid, diplomacy, trade, defence and soft-power instruments such as the Australian Broadcasting Corporation. And most critically, that these tools are supported, not undermined, by Australia's domestic policy.

Paul Ronalds is chief executive officer of Save the Children Australia

Carlisle Richardson

n "Cross Purposes", Jenny Hayward-Jones proposes that Australia's declining influence in the Pacific is a result of divergent views over security and climate change, along with the rise of China as a rival player in the region. These have been significant factors, yet there is another that supersedes all else. Identity determines the strength or weakness of Australia's relationship with its Pacific neighbours, and this aspect requires more attention than Hayward-Jones gives it.

Australia's Pacific past includes being an administering power during the colonial period, which still has an impact on its identity in the region. Economic disparities separate it further from Pacific island nations and, as it is a more developed country, give it an alternative worldview. Despite attempts from Australia to produce a shared identity as "custodians of the Pacific Ocean", these distinctions continue to determine the manner in which Australia and Pacific nations interact. Australia still views itself as the leader in the region, but leadership is not primarily what those in the Pacific islands are seeking from their neighbour.

Hayward-Jones correctly characterises climate change as an existential issue for Pacific islanders – something that has not been fully grasped by Australia. The recent assertion of a climate emergency by Pacific island nations in the 2019 Nadi Bay Declaration, as well as the outcome of the recent Pacific Islands Forum, showed the widening gap in positions between Australia and the Pacific.

Australia has yet to determine its identity when it comes to its Pacific neighbours. It fluctuates between a relationship of *vuvale* (family), as Scott Morrison expressed it recently, and benefactor – though one whose benevolence towards the Pacific comes with the expectation of support for its priorities. For instance, Papua New Guinea became independent from Australia in 1975 but remains among the largest recipients of Australian aid. Psychologically, the colonial trappings remain. Accordingly to many in Papua New Guinea, Canberra has exhibited indifference to its concerns, such as climate change, yet pressures Port Moresby to align with its priorities, such as security. Papua New Guinea's flirtation with China can thus be interpreted as a desire to no longer be beholden and indebted to Australia. China presents an opportunity for economic and foreign policy independence.

There are echoes of this across the Pacific. While other Pacific island nations were not colonies of Australia, the ambiguity of the relationship has prompted them to follow a similar path. The conclusion among Pacific island nations is that if a genuine familial bond existed, Australia would pay greater attention to addressing their climate concerns. That explains why such countries would seek alliances elsewhere.

Hayward-Jones discusses Australia's aid program and suggests that, while there were no overt directives, the aid could be interpreted as an incentive to fall in line. This is the crux of the problem. No sovereign country with its own proud history wants to be led. Simmering resentments fester and rise when differences, such as on climate change, occur.

In a shifting international environment, Australia will have to reassess its regional self-image. This will influence its climate policy and its handling of the regional jostling with China. Ultimately, Australia cannot assume that its neighbours will simply follow its lead. There will have to be a recognition that the Pacific islands are not "aid clients with limited agency" but rather equal partners with shared values, separate identities and their own regional priorities.

Carlisle Richardson is a former UN ambassador of St Kitts and Nevis

Jenny Hayward-Jones responds

The three responses to my essay agree on a central point: Australia's inability to recognise that climate change poses an existential threat to Pacific island countries and to act on that recognition damages its relations with its Pacific neighbours. This point was made obvious during the leaders' summit at the Pacific Islands Forum (PIF) in Tuvalu in August, when a dispute between Australia and Pacific island countries over the language used on climate change and coal in the communiqué and in the accompanying statement, the Kainaki II Declaration for Urgent Climate Change Action Now, amplified the rift. A comment by Deputy Prime Minister Michael McCormack at a business function, suggesting that Pacific islanders could survive the climate emergency by participating in seasonal work schemes in Australia, was a regrettable demonstration of the Australian government's indifference to the plight of the Pacific islands.

Sandra Tarte believes it is time for the PIF to frame climate change as an existential threat to all its members, including Australia. It is difficult to see how Australia can reconcile its differences over climate change policy with Pacific island countries under the Morrison government, or while the coal industry is regarded as vital to Australia's economic fortunes. But Scott Morrison's efforts to publicly support the "Pacific step-up" and engage with his counterparts, including by making five trips to the region and hosting a high-profile visit by new Papua New Guinean prime minister James Marape, indicate that he understands the need to repair the rift.

Tarte is right to warn that Canberra, in the midst of its hand-wringing about the growing influence of China, tends to ignore the agency of Pacific island countries. Australia's desire to continue to outspend China in aid and financing and to assert its military dominance in the region suggests that it wants to curtail China's presence and make Pacific island governments choose it over China. Tarte, correctly, suggests this creates a false dichotomy. Australia seems unwilling to acknowledge that just as it manages relations with a principal trading partner (China) that is a strategic adversary and with a principal security partner (the United States) that is increasingly unpredictable, Pacific island countries are independent states that can manage relations with larger powers with differing priorities.

In my essay, I argue that policy differences on climate change have damaged Australia's relations with the region. Paul Ronalds points out that a lack of coherence in Australia's foreign and domestic policies has also distorted and undermined Australia's very significant aid program in the Pacific. He argues that Australia's aid could have been focused more usefully on improving health outcomes for Papua New Guineans rather than diverted to causes supporting Australia's offshore processing deals with Papua New Guinea and Nauru – an unfortunate example of Australia's domestic politics undermining its foreign policy. Ronalds suggests that the proposed Australian Infrastructure Financing Facility for the Pacific, which will be funded in part from the aid program, will also result in missed opportunities to address major problems such as endemic violence and chronic childhood malnutrition in Papua New Guinea. I concur with his critique of Australia's priorities. Australia's desire to match whatever China offers the region may see it lose focus on what is really important for Pacific islanders.

Carlisle Richardson contends that Australia has yet to determine its identity when it comes to its Pacific neighbours. I agree, and accept Richardson's criticism that I did not give sufficient attention to the question of identity. Australia's size, economy and societal make-up differ greatly from those of Pacific island countries and, as Richardson says, it has a different worldview. As I note in my essay, Australia worries that Pacific island states do not understand the threat posed by China, and Pacific island states worry that Australia does not understand the threat posed by climate change. But I do not agree with Richardson that Australia's identity problem supersedes all other factors in determining the strength or weakness of its relationships with its Pacific neighbours.

Australia, as a Western nation much larger than its island neighbours, cannot easily change its identity. Unlike New Zealand, Australia does not have a large Pacific population to help it identify with its Pacific neighbours. Its reliance on fossil fuel exports and the reluctance of the political class to embrace the commitments required to address the climate emergency put it at odds with Pacific island states. And as I argue in my essay, Australia's security interests are different from those of Pacific island countries. Australia's domestic experience of the negative impact of Chinese influence, combined with growing anxiety about the threat China poses to peace and stability in the wider Pacific region that has been underpinned by the United States for more than seventy years, makes Canberra justifiably nervous about China's intentions.

But this difference in identity should not prevent the Australian government from showing empathy with its Pacific counterparts, recognising the separate national priorities of island countries or acknowledging that climate change is an existential threat, as well as the primary security threat to the region. It should not have prevented the exercise of much better diplomacy in negotiating with other members of the PIF in Tuvalu. And it should not prevent Australia from taking more substantial measures to increase financing for adaptation and mitigation programs, or its political leaders from showing respect for Pacific island peoples. Australia may never have a shared identity with Pacific island states or be accepted as part of the Pacific family, but it can change its attitude and still be a valuable partner for countries in the region.

Jenny Hayward-Jones is a non-resident fellow at the Lowy Institute

Subscribe to Australian Foreign Affairs & save up to 28% on the cover price.

Enjoy free home delivery of the print edition and full digital as well as ebook access to the journal via the Australian Foreign Affairs website, iPad, iPhone and Android apps.

Forthcoming issue:
Can We Trust America?
(February 2020)

Never miss an issue. Subscribe and save.

☐ **1 year auto-renewing print and digital subscription** (3 issues) $49.99 within Australia. Outside Australia $79.99*.

☐ **1 year print and digital subscription** (3 issues) $59.99 within Australia. Outside Australia $99.99.

☐ **1 year auto-renewing digital subscription** (3 issues) $29.99.*

☐ **2 year print and digital subscription** (6 issues) $114.99 within Australia.

☐ Tick here to commence subscription with the current issue.

Give an inspired gift. Subscribe a friend.

☐ **1 year print and digital gift subscription** (3 issues) $59.99 within Australia. Outside Australia $99.99.

☐ **1 year digital-only gift subscription** (3 issues) $29.99.

☐ **2 year print and digital gift subscription** (6 issues) $114.99 within Australia.

☐ Tick here to commence subscription with the current issue.

ALL PRICES INCLUDE GST, POSTAGE AND HANDLING.

*Your subscription will automatically renew until you notify us to stop. Prior to the end of your subscription period, we will send you a reminder notice.

Please turn over for subscription order form, or subscribe online at **australianforeignaffairs.com**
Alternatively, call 1800 077 514 or +61 3 9486 0288 or email **subscribe@australianforeignaffairs.com**

Back Issues

ALL PRICES INCLUDE
GST, POSTAGE
AND HANDLING.

☐ **AFA1** ($15.99)
The Big Picture

☐ **AFA2** ($15.99)
Trump in Asia

☐ **AFA3** ($15.99)
Australia & Indonesia

☐ **AFA4** ($15.99)
Defending Australia

☐ **AFA5** ($22.99)
Are We Asian Yet?

☐ **AFA6** ($22.99)
Our Sphere of Influence

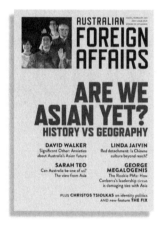

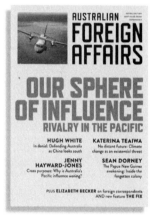

PAYMENT DETAILS I enclose a cheque/money order made out to Schwartz Books Pty Ltd.
Or please debit my credit card (MasterCard, Visa or Amex accepted).

CARD NO. ☐☐☐☐ ☐☐☐☐ ☐☐☐☐ ☐☐☐☐

EXPIRY DATE _____ / _____ CCV _____ AMOUNT $ _____

CARDHOLDER'S NAME _____

SIGNATURE _____

NAME _____

ADDRESS _____

_____

EMAIL _____ PHONE _____

Post or fax this form to: Reply Paid 90094, Carlton VIC 3053 **Freecall:** 1800 077 514 **or** +61 3 9486 0288
Fax: (03) 9011 6106 **Email:** subscribe@australianforeignaffairs.com **Website:** australianforeignaffairs.com
Subscribe online at australianforeignaffairs.com/subscribe (please do not send electronic scans of this form)

Until Sunday, 3 November 2019, we are open for submissions on the topic of this issue, *China Dependence*, to be published on the Australian Foreign Affairs website.

NEXT 💬
VOICES

The best new thinkers on Australian foreign affairs

Contributions must be 1500–2000 words and previously unpublished. Authors whose work is selected will receive A$100 and a one-year print and digital subscription to Australian Foreign Affairs, and will collaborate with Australian Foreign Affairs editors to shape and refine their piece.

Writers do not have to be foreign-affairs experts: journalists, academics, foreign-aid workers, policy advisers, students and other interested readers are encouraged to submit. We seek to foster and promote a diverse stable of writers from Australia and the Asia-Pacific, and to encourage discussion on foreign affairs that represents a range of views in the broader Australian community.

To read our guidelines and submit,
visit **australianforeignaffairs.com/next-voices**

The Back Page

INDO-PACIFIC

What is it: A geopolitical construct that links two oceans, the Indian and the Pacific. The 2012 White Paper "Australia in the Asian Century" used the term, apparently reflecting a change in strategy – encompassing more "Indo-" and less "Asia-", or more India and less China. According to Rory Medcalf (professor, Australian National University), "leaders and senior policy figures from Australia, India, Indonesia, Japan and the United States are increasingly using the term" to describe the regional order.

Where did it come from: Relative obscurity. Captain Gurpreet Khurana (executive director, National Maritime Foundation), a former ship's diver in the Indian navy, first explained the concept in a paper in 2007 called "Security of Sea Lines: Prospects for India–Japan Cooperation". Soon after, Shinzō Abe (prime minister, Japan) began using the term, to widespread attention.

Is it sticking: So far. On his 2017 trip to Asia, Donald Trump (president, United States) used the term repeatedly, without referring to the Asia-Pacific once.

What does China think: China has made few official responses, but Wang Yi (foreign minister, People's Republic of China) is unhappy with the term. "There's never a shortage of headline-grabbing ideas, but they are like sea foam in the Pacific or Indian Ocean," he told reporters. "They may get some attention but will be short-lived."

Does it actually exist: While the Indo-Pacific "has a maritime security rationale, its economic logic remains under-developed", according to Jeffrey D. Wilson (research director, Perth USAsia Centre).

More hyphens please: In 2013, some US foreign affairs gurus began referring to the "Indo-Asia-Pacific".